SUPER
SMART

SUPER SMART

180 Challenging Thinking Activities, Words, and Ideas for Advanced Students

by

Stephen S. Young

DISCARD

PRUFROCK PRESS INC. • WACO, TEXAS

Edited by Jennifer Robins, Layout Design by Marjorie Parker

Library of Congress Cataloging-in-Publication Data

Young, Stephen S., 1943-
    Super smart : 180 challenging thinking activities, words, and ideas for advanced students / by
    Stephen S. Young.
        p. cm.
    ISBN 1-59363-155-3 (pbk.)
    1. Literary recreations. 2. Educational games. I. Title.
    GV1493.Y68 2005
    371.33'7—dc22
                                                  2005018378

Printed in the United States of America.

ISBN 1-59363-155-3

Prufrock Press, Inc.
P.O. Box 8813
Waco, Texas 76714-8813
(800) 998-2208
Fax (800) 240-0333
http://www.prufrock.com

Contents

Introduction

Okay, let's get to it. No theory, studies, lectures, or advice. You're a teacher, and you're looking for ways to get your class off to a better start each day.

Since most school systems base their school year on 180 days, I have collected a hook or grabber with which you can start each day. The term *hook* or *grabber* is synonymous with a short, attention-getting device, object, activity, or experience that serves to hook or grab the students' attention and create a frame of mind and an atmosphere of fun, curiosity, or discovery conducive to getting the lesson off to a good start.

There are three hooks for each day: a word game, a thought for the day, and a hook designed to get students thinking and into a receptive mind set. You can use most of the hooks without preparation, but a few do need to be prepared or practiced first.

The **Word for the Day** can be written on the board. Read the four possible definitions and have the students vote for the definition they think is the correct one. You then reveal the correct definition. If you wish, you can even divide the class into teams and keep score over the course of the year or grading period and give a prize to the team with the most points, or you can simply make it a little competitive game between you and them, you trying to fool them into selecting an incorrect answer while they try to cut through your smoke screens.

The **Thought for the Day** is simply an adage, some from famous historical characters, some from that guy anon, some humorous, some serious, but all designed to give the student pause. To assure they have the correct interpretation, you may wish to have a student paraphrase the quote and/or explain what it means—but don't get too academic about it. Keep it light and fun.

The **Critical Thinking Hook**, while short, may take a bit more time than the word or thought (the three together will not take more than 5–7 minutes). It can be introduced at the beginning of class with the answer revealed just before class is over, or you can carry it over to the next day if no one has gotten the answer. You won't want to provide the answer, but rather have the students figure it out for themselves.

These are just suggestions. You know your students, so use these hooks and grabbers in the manner that works best for you.

A question that always arises: Does the hook or grabber have to be related to today's lesson? Absolutely *not*. If, by coincidence, one is related, so much the better, but the hook or grabber is a motivational/critical thinking device first and foremost. If it does nothing more than pique their curiosity, tickle their funny bone, arouse their sense of justice, or simply create an atmosphere in which they feel more comfortable, challenged, and worthy, the hook or grabber will have accomplished its task.

I have included a variety of examples of hooks and grabbers that I have written and collected. Many have been brought to me by my students over the years. I have tried to give credit where the known source of the hook could be identified. Many of these have been brought to me or collected through word of mouth, so if I have inadvertently failed to give proper credit, I apologize and will be glad to make the necessary corrections in later editions.

Warning: Use the right terminology, as I once had a student, who had prepared a reflective teaching exercise, approach me on Monday morning after class had started and announce, "Dr. Young, I looked all weekend and couldn't find a hooker anywhere!" There was a noticeable silence in the room until I replied, "Have you tried the corner of Third and Rose?" at which time the class broke up and the red-faced young man also suddenly saw the error of his linguistic ways.

So good luck with these *hooks* or *grabbers* . . . but watch out for those *hookers*, they'll get you in trouble every time.

—SSY

Day 1

Word of the Day:

admonition (ad´ mo nish´ on)

A. A mild cautionary rebuke or warning (noun)
B. An award for bravery or honor
C. An advertisement or promotional statement
D. An admission of failure

Derivatives: admonish, admonitor, admonitory, admonishment, admonisher
Use: The investors did not heed his *admonition*, deciding to buy the risky stock anyway.

Thought of the Day:

"Kindness consists in loving people more than they deserve." *Joubert*

Hook:

Without lifting pencil from paper, draw no more than four straight lines so that each dot in the figure is intersected by a line. You may not retrace any lines.

Solution:

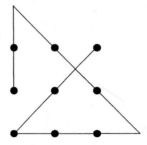

No one said you couldn't draw beyond the points. Actually, there are several ways to do it. The illustration is just one.

Day 2

Word of the Day:

quid pro quo (kwid´ pro kwo´)

A Latin phrase meaning:

(A.) An equal exchange (noun)
B. Uninformed
C. Illegal
D. Accepted by the majority

Use: The teacher and students arrived at a *quid pro quo*, the students being allowed to talk quietly with each other as long as they completed their assignment.

Thought of the Day:

"I love most my best friend *and* my bravest enemy for it is they who keep me keenly honed and to the mark." *G. B. Shaw*

Hook:

The following words can be manipulated in such a way as to achieve a rather unusual effect. What is the manipulation and the effect?

BULL, BIG, PECK, LOST, PAT

Solution:

You can substitute any vowel within each word and it will still form a real word (e.g., ball, bell, bill, boll, bull).

Day 3

Word of the Day:

prognosticate (prog nos´ ta kate)

A. To delay or stall for time
B. To expel from the throat
C. To make excuses
D. To predict (verb)

Derivatives: prognosis, prognostic, prognostication, prognosticator
Use: The so-called psychic failed badly at trying to *prognosticate* the client's future.

Thought of the Day:

"Guys will forgive a woman for absolutely anything, except outwitting them." *Anon*

Hook:

There are three light switches on a hallway wall outside a room. Two of the switches are dummies connected to nothing. The other switch is wired to an outlet in the room into which a lamp is plugged. The lamp switch is turned on, but the lamp will not light until the correct switch is thrown on the hallway wall. The door to the room is closed and the keyhole and crack under the door are plugged. You cannot in any way see into the room.

You may manipulate the three switches in any manner you wish and only then may you open the door and enter the room. Once you have entered the room you must immediately determine which of the three switches is the hot one (wired to the outlet). You may not manipulate the switches once you have entered the room.

How do you determine which is the hot switch?

Solution:

Start with all three switches in the off position. Turn the first switch on for five minutes then turn it off. Immediately turn on the second switch. Now enter the room. If the lamp is lit, the second switch that you just turned on is the correct one. If the lamp is not lit, walk over and feel the bulb. If it is warm, the first switch is the correct one. If the bulb is cool, the third switch is the hot one.

Thanks to Stephanie Ferguson for this hook.

Day 4

Word of the Day:

pugnacious (pug na´ shus)

(A.) Quarrelsome (adj.)
B. Flat-nosed
C. Stubborn
D. Pregnant

Derivatives: pugnacity, pugnaciousness, pugnaciously

Use: His *pugnacious* nature led us to try working with other members of the staff who were more cooperative.

Thought of the Day:

"Take risks! You cannot discover new oceans unless you have the courage to lose sight of the shore." *Anon*

Hook:

The following is a rebus (a graphic representation of a well-known title, quote, phrase, adage, or proverb). To interpret it, you must decipher the words and symbols (think outside the box—look for alternative meanings) and come up with the answer.

ooooooohs and

Solution:

First line: The expression is ooooooohs and ahhhhhhs, but the ahhhhhhs are missing so we have "no ahhhhhhs."

Second line: This type of line segment is called an arc.

So the solution to the rebus is: no ahhhhhhs arc (Noah's ark).

Day 5

Word of the Day:

pejorative (pe jor´ a tiv)

A. Clumsy or awkward
B. Vomit inducing
C. Disparaging or downgrading (adj.)
D. Hopeful, optimistic

Derivatives: pejoration, pejoratively
Use: Her continual *pejorative* remarks made it clear she would not support the proposal.

Thought of the Day:

"If the crow could just feed quietly, it would have more to eat." *Horace*

Hook:

How about three humorous riddles to start the day?

1. What do you call a woodland aquatic creature who should reconsider the wisdom of his actions?

2. What do you call a large swimming mammal who dirties kitchen utensils?

3. What do you call a large reptile who tells tall tales on the telephone?

Solution:

1. An "otter not do that."

2. A "hippo-pot-a-mess."

3. A "crock-a-dial."

Day 6

Word of the Day:

solicitous (so lis´ i tus)

- A. Requesting a favor
- B. Wishing to be left alone
- (C.) Attentive, concerned (adj.)
- D. Absent

Derivative: solicitude

Use: We were pleasantly surprised to find the whole committee *solicitous* during our entire presentation.

Thought of the Day:

"The mind of the bigot is like the pupil of the eye; the more light you cast upon it, the more it contracts." *Oliver Wendell Holmes*

Hook:

A man carrying *three* crystal balls approached a bridge. The bridge was old and ready to collapse. It could support only the weight of the man and two of the crystal balls. The bridge was too long for the man to throw or roll the balls across, yet he was able to get all three crystal balls across in only one trip. How did he do it?

Hint:

He was a circus performer.

Solution:

He juggled them while walking across, keeping one ball in the air at all times.

Day7

Word of the Day:

sequester (se kwes´ ter)

A. To run a high fever
(B.) To remove and hold in isolation (verb)
C. A term from the middle ages meaning ⅛ of a mile
(D.) To requisition and confiscate property (verb)

Derivatives: sequestrant, sequestrate, sequestration, sequestrum
Use #1: Unfortunately, we will have to *sequester* the jury for at least 3 weeks.
Use #2: Because the man refused to sell the 40 acres needed for the new highway project, the county was forced to *sequester* his property.

Thought of the Day:

"Happiness is not a reward and suffering is not a punishment—rather they are both consequences." *Robert Green Ingersoll*

Hook:

Write the following on the board, project it on a screen, or distribute it as a handout exactly as it is written below.

This is an unusual paragraph. I'm curious how quickly you can find out what is so unusual about it. It looks so plain you would think nothing is wrong with it. In fact, nothing is wrong with it! It is unusual, though. You may study it and think about it, but not find anything odd or out of position. But if you work at it a bit, you might find a solution to this foxy conundrum. Good luck!

Hint:

There is something missing from the paragraph.

Solution:

The entire paragraph is written without using the letter "e."

Day8

Word of the Day:

diaphanous (di af´ a nus)

A. Translucent, transparent (adj.)
B. Made of extremely thin material
C. Having two distinct points of view
D. Villainous, underhanded

Derivatives: diaphaneity, diaphanousness, diaphanously
Use: Because the bag in which she kept the secret was *diaphanous*, Barbara's secret did not stay a secret very long.

Thought of the Day:

"There are two important aims in life: First, get what you want and after that, enjoy it. Many achieve the first, but only the wisest achieve the second." *L. P. Smith*

Hook:

You receive a mysterious letter in the mail that says: **The Reds will beat the Dodgers next Tuesday.** You figure "no way" because the Reds are having an off year. Yet, on Tuesday the Reds do win. Lucky guess, you think.

A few days later another cryptic letter arrives with the prediction: **The Twins will defeat the Yankees on Saturday.** Now you know this guy is crazy because the Twins are in the cellar and the Yankees are leading their division, yet on Saturday the Twins win on a ninth inning homer.

You wonder.

A few days later comes a third letter. **The Padres will beat the Cubs on Monday night,** it says, and again you wonder because the Cubs have been hot and the Padres are mired near the bottom of their division. Yet again, there is an upset with the Padres winning 6–3.

A fourth letter arrives stating, **the Brewers will defeat the Marlins on Wednesday.** Again, the mysterious prognosticator is predicting a major upset. The Marlins are defending champions and the Brewers have a losing record with weak hitting and bad pitching. You watch the game on TV with astonishment on Wednesday as the Brewers win 12–3.

The mysterious letter writer has now hit four in a row, all upsets that should not have happened. In the mail comes a fifth letter: **If you want my next pick, send $100 to P.O. Box 55.**

With a sure thing, you could lay down some bets and make a bundle. Do you send him the $100?

Solution:

Not on your life, because your guess is as good as his! Here's the scam he's running: He started with the addresses of, say, 100 people. He had no idea who would actually win, but he sent 50 of those people a letter predicting a Reds victory and 50 a letter predicting a Dodgers victory. When the Reds won, he took those 50 people and sent 25 a second letter picking the Twins and 25 a letter picking the Yankees. When the Twins won, he took those 25 people and sent 12 a letter picking the Padres and 13 a letter picking the Cubs. When the Padres won, he took those 12 people and sent 6 a letter predicting a Brewers victory and 6 a letter predicting the Marlins would win. When the Brewers won, he took those 6 people and sent them the letter asking for $100 for his next pick. If you were unlucky enough to be one of those six, you might think this guy can really pick them when, in reality, he has no idea who will win. So if you pay your $100, he may give you a pick, but it will only be a guess and don't be surprised if it's wrong (the chances are 50/50). You might as well flip a coin. That's probably what the prognosticator will do. You may bet a bundle on his prediction and lose, and he's got your $100.

Be careful: This scam is probably legal. If he provides the prediction, he has given you what he promised for your money. He has offered no guarantee of being correct, only that he would provide a prediction. If he sends you that prediction (right or wrong), he has fulfilled his part of the agreement and is probably beyond prosecution.

Day9

Word of the Day:

tantamount (tan´ ta mount)

- A. Large, overwhelming
- B. A large square tent open on one side
- C. Equivalent to, virtually the same (adj.)
- D. The winch that raises or lowers a ship's anchor

Use: His unwillingness to contradict the accusation was *tantamount* to a confession.

Thought of the Day:

"The only sin which we never forgive in each other is a difference of opinion." *Emerson*

Hook:

You have five sections of chain as seen below. You wish to combine them into one long chain. This is accomplished by cutting a link, slipping it through, and closing the link again. The cutting and closing of a link is one operation. What is the fewest number of operations necessary to create one long chain?

Solution:

It can be done in only three operations. To do it, break all three links in one section and use them to join the other four sections.

Day 10

Word of the Day:

opprobrious (a pro´ bree us)

A. Pertaining to the allocation of monetary funds
B. Well suited, capable
C. Shameful, infamous (adj.)
D. Overflowing with gratitude

Derivatives: opprobriously, opprobrium

Use: His *opprobrious* behavior, which caused a great deal of embarrassment, gave us reason to question why we had asked him to join our group in the first place.

Thought of the Day:

"Life is full of choices. Three good ones: Choose life! Choose love! Choose action!" *Anon*

Hook:

How about a card trick? This one is easy and works itself. Give a deck of cards to a student. Turn your back and have the student select any 10 cards from the deck. Then have the student turn those cards face up and reinsert them anywhere into the deck. They can be reinserted all together or individually placed in different parts of the deck. Now, the rest of the deck is face down except for the 10 cards. Make a big deal of your magical powers and ask the class if they think you can, without touching or even seeing the deck, divide the deck into two piles that will have an equal number of cards face up. They will, of course, say "no way."

Have the student with the cards count off the top 10 cards from the deck. They may or may not contain one or more of the 10 face up cards—it doesn't matter. Have the student turn over those 10 cards. Next, have the student count the number of cards facing up in that pile of 10. Now, have the student go through the rest of the deck and count the number of face up cards. Magically, the two numbers will be the same (and always will be). Ta-da!

Solution:

(See if the students can figure this out for themselves.) Let's assume after the selection, reinsertion, and dealing of the top 10 cards that there are now 3 cards face up in that pile of 10. That leaves 7 face up cards in the rest of the deck. By turning over the pile of 10, you have created the reciprocal or complement of those original 3 cards. You now have 7 cards face up in the pile of 10, which will automatically equal the number of face up cards in the rest of the deck.

Day 11

Word of the Day:

sedulous (sed´ u lus)

- A. Argumentative
- B. Rebellious
- C. Credible, believable
- (D.) Industrious (adj.)

Derivatives: sedulousness, sedulously
Use: It is obvious, that with such a *sedulous* demeanor, Jones will go far in the company.

Thought of the Day:

"Stick with people who make you laugh. They are much less expensive than a therapist." *Anon*

Hook:

Write, duplicate, or project the following paragraph, exactly as shown, and have the students read it.

Aoccdrnig to rscheearch at Cmabgrigde Uinervtisy teh oredr of ltteers in a wrod deosn't mttaer. The olny iprmoatnt tihng is taht the frist and lsat ltteer be at the rghit pclae. The rset can be a toatl mses and you can sitll raed it wouthit a porbelm. Tihs is bcuseae the huamn mnid deos not raed ervey lteter by istlef, but the wrod as a wlohe.

Rather amazing. It also at least partially explains why proofreading is so difficult. The mind interprets the word correctly even though it may be misspelled.

Day 12

Word of the Day:

rapacious (ra pay´ shus)

A. Raptor-like, preying on others (adj.)
B. Outgoing, personable
C. Argumentative
D. Stingy, penny pinching

Derivatives: rapaciousness, rapacity, rapaciously
Use: She may seem to have your best interests at heart, but her *rapacious* nature will surface sooner or later.

Thought of the Day:

"Luck sometimes visits a fool, but never sits down with him." *Proverb*

Hook:

This may sound like math, but it simply requires some analysis.

Bob and Larry run the 100-yard dash. Bob wins by 10 yards. They decide to race again, but this time Bob says that in order to make the race more fair, he will start 10 yards behind the starting line. They race again. Assuming each runs at the same speed that he did the first time, who wins? Bob? Larry? Or do they tie?

Solution:

Bob wins again. Since Bob can cover 100 yards in the same time Larry covers only 90, Bob will run the 10 yards to the starting line and an additional 90 yards in the same time Larry covers 90 yards from the starting line. This means that at the 90 yard mark they will be even and since Bob is the faster runner, he will win again. What will his winning margin be the second time? One yard, since he covers that last 10 yards in the same time Larry covers only 9.

Day 13

Word of the Day:

ligature (lig´ a tur)

A. Bonds used to tie or bind (noun)
B. Connective tissue around joints
C. Pertaining to the legality of an action
D. An X used as a substitute for a signature

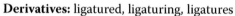

Derivatives: ligatured, ligaturing, ligatures
Use: No matter how hard he struggled, his *ligatures* held him tightly bound.

Thought of the Day:

"Some like to understand what they believe in. Others like to believe in what they understand." *Anon*

Hook:

The game is called NYM and is played by two people at a time. The object is to be the first player to reach 17. The two players count upwards starting at one. Each player may increase the count by one or by two. For instance, player one starts and may say "one" or "one, two," whereupon player two picks up the count by adding one or two. If player one stopped at "two," player two could say, "three" or "three, four," whereupon it would be player one's turn again. The exchange of turns continues until someone reaches 17. Knowing the strategy will ensure you win every time. Play a few rounds and see if a strategy emerges.

Solution:

To arrive at 17, you must hit 14 because no matter if your opponent says "15" or "15, 16," you can reach 17. To insure you get to 14, the magic number is 11. To get to 11, you must hit 8. To get to 8, your magic number is 5, and to reach 5 the magic number is 2. Which means, if you start and say "one, two," regardless of what your opponent does, you have won the game by hitting each of those *magic* numbers (*intervals of three, counting down from 17*). So, 2, 5, 8, 11, and 14 are the numbers you want to hit. You can even let your opponent go first. If he or she hasn't figured out the system, your opponent will probably not stop on the entire sequence of magic numbers. When that happens, you jump onto any magic number along the way and you have won.

I used this game for more than 2 weeks with my classes before they caught on. I would play one and only one round of NYM each morning. Of course I would always win and they would accuse me of cheating and I would tell them, "Of *course* I'm cheating, but *how* am I doing it?" Eventually they figured it out, but it was great fun.

Day 14

Word of the Day:

soporific (sop or if´ ik)

A. Exceptionally good or of the highest quality
B. Overly emotional or sentimental
C. Immature, not well thought out
D. Sleep inducing (adj.)

Derivatives: soporiferous, soporiferously, soporiferousness

Use: The nature of John's report was interesting, but with his *soporific* monotone, my attention kept drifting and I had trouble keeping my eyes open.

Thought of the Day:

"In the first place God made idiots—that was for practice. Then He made Congress." Attributed to *Mark Twain*—but then isn't just about everything?

Hook:

Read to the class: Three men check into a second-rate hotel. The hotel manager indicates that there is only one room left, and asked if they would be willing to share the room. The three agree. The manager says that while the room is normally $30 per night, he will let them have it for $27. Each man forks over $9, and they proceed to the room. A while later the manager concludes that because the room is small and all three men will be forced to share that small space, he did not deduct enough off the normal rate. So he calls the bellboy, gives him five $1 bills and tells him to give each man a refund. The bellboy, on his way to the room, ponders how he can divide $5 among three men. Having no means of making change, he simply knocks on the door, gives each man $1 as a refund and pockets the other two dollar bills for himself.

Here's the conundrum: If each man gets a dollar bill back, this means each man is now paying only $8 for the room. Three times eight is $24, plus the $2 the bellboy kept, which makes a total of $26. Since they had originally paid $27 for the room, what happened to the other dollar?

Solution:

It is easy to see that the hotel had $27 of the men's money to begin with. Take away the $3 that was refunded and you have $24. Take away the $2 the bellboy kept and you now have the hotel making only $22 on the transaction. Now reverse the process and it will indeed add up to $27. But that is not what was called for. What was called for was to point out the fallacy behind the original reasoning. I have talked with a number of mathematicians and about all they will say is, "You can't figure it that way." OK, why not? You might want to refer the students to the math teacher on this one (this will make you very popular with the math teacher).

Day 15

Word of the Day:

modicum (mod´ i cum)

- (A.) A moderate amount (noun)
- B. A soothing ointment
- C. The leader or moderator of a discussion
- D. A microphone used to record extremely low
  volume sounds

Use: Despite being filled with facts, the research paper contained only a *modicum* of useful information.

Thought of the Day:

"Advice is a lot like medicine. You have to take it before it can do you any good." *Anon*

Hook:

You have two identical beakers, each holding an identical amount of fluid. One beaker holds red fluid, the other blue fluid. You take 1 tablespoon of the red fluid, drop it into the blue fluid and mix it up thoroughly. You then take 1 tablespoon of this mixture, drop it back into the red fluid and mix it up thoroughly. Question: Do you now have more red fluid in the predominantly blue beaker, more blue fluid in the predominantly red beaker, or are there equal amounts in each?

Solution:

Equal amounts. Although the quantity in each beaker is irrelevant, let us assume, that, to begin with, each beaker has 9 tablespoons of fluid. In step one we transfer 1 tablespoon of red fluid to the blue beaker. We now have 10 tablespoons of fluid in that beaker, one-tenth of which is red and nine-tenths of which is blue. We now transfer 1 tablespoon of that mixture back into the red beaker. That tablespoon is one-tenth red and nine-tenths blue, so we have actually transferred one-tenth of a tablespoon of red fluid *back into* the red container, making the net amount of red fluid left in the blue container nine-tenths of a tablespoon. When we transferred the mixture into the red container, that tablespoon was one-tenth red and nine-tenths blue, so the net amount of blue we transferred into the red container was also nine-tenths of a tablespoon. Not as easy as it seemed at first, eh?

Day 16

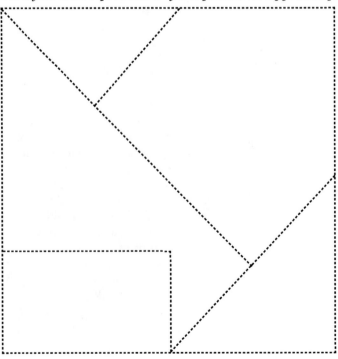

Word of the Day:

gregarious (gree gar´ e us)

A. Confident
B. Sociable (adj.)
C. Full of holes
D. Selfish

Derivatives: gregariousness, gregariously
Use: Even though she was new at school, with her *gregarious* personality, Janet made friends very quickly.

Thought of the Day:
Hook:

"One hour in doing justice is worth a hundred in prayer." *Mahomet*

Below is a conventional five piece puzzle. Cut along the lines to create the five pieces. Use a material that is the same on both front and back (makes it harder when you don't know if you have the piece right side up). It looks simple now with the pieces in place, but not so easy when you don't have the solution in front of you. You might want to create four or five sets of puzzle pieces and let the students play in teams to see who can be first to use *all five* pieces to form a square:

For a full-sized reproducible of this puzzle, see Appendix, page 208.

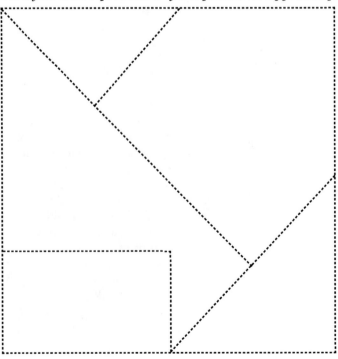

Day 17

Word of the Day:

nefarious (nee fair´ e us)

A. Evil, infamous (adj.)
B. Unreasonable
C. Mysterious
D. In a speedy manner

Derivatives: nefariously, nefariousness
Use: His *nefarious* reputation made him a suspect from the very beginning.

Thought of the Day:

"Logical consequences are the scarecrows of fools and the beacons of those who are wise." *Huxley*

Hook:

A logic puzzle: Write A–D below on the board or projector, and read the following: ***All the secretaries who work in my office are under 25 years of age and are quite attractive. My office secretary has long blonde hair and blue eyes.*** Which of the following statements can be correctly inferred from the statements above?

A. My secretary is under 25 years of age.
B. My secretary is an attractive woman.
C. Both A and B above are true.
D. Neither A nor B above is true.

Solution:

A. *All* the secretaries are under 25, so my secretary must also be under 25. Why not B? Because it is possible that I might have a long-haired, blue-eyed, attractive, *male* secretary. Tricky? Of course! That's what makes it fun and requires your students to read carefully, without making unwarranted assumptions.

Day 18

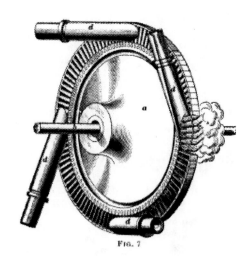

FIG. 7

Word of the Day:

machinate (mac´ i nate)

A. To use a machine or device
B. To plot or scheme (verb)
C. A bitter tropical fruit
D. To debate endlessly

Derivatives: machination, machinated, machinating, machinates, machinator
Use: The three conspirators withdrew to the back room to *machinate* their attempt to take control of the assembly.

Thought of the Day:

"Life is a little gleam of time between two eternities. There is no second chance." *Thomas Carlyle*

Hook:

Another rebus to decode:

Forwar
Pas

Solution:

An incomplete forward pass.

Day 19

Word of the Day:

inception (in cep´ shun)

(A.) The start or beginning (noun)
B. A misunderstanding
C. A sudden inspiration
D. A basic truth

Derivative: inceptive
Use: From its very *inception*, we knew the plan was doomed to fail.

Thought of the Day:

"Most history is simply gossip which has grown old gracefully." *Sidney Harris*

Hook:

Using standard 8 ½" x 11" paper, cut 2-inch strips lengthwise. This will give you four strips per piece of paper. The last one will be a little wider. Give each student a strip of paper and a challenge. Tell them you will give them only 1 minute to draw a single continuous line on both sides of the paper without lifting the pencil from the paper and without going over an edge. They, of course, will be unable to do this and will declare it impossible. Now give them a second strip of paper and a small piece of tape. Instruct them to hold each end of the paper in a separate hand, and rotate one end of the paper only so that they put a half twist in it. Now instruct them to bring the two ends of the strip together and tape them. The resulting paper now looks like this:

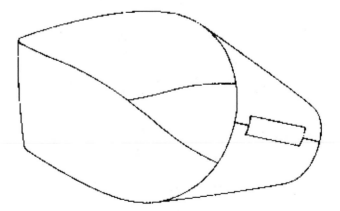

This strange-looking critter is called a Möbius Strip. Now have each student place the Möbius Strip on the desk and place his or her pencil point on the part of the strip lying in contact with the desk. Keeping the pencil where it is, drag the strip under the pencil with the free hand. Continue doing this until, voilà, the pencil arrives back where it started. If the student takes the strip apart again, he or she will find a continuous line on both sides of the paper. Have the students put the strip back together. Ask them how many sides a Möbius Strip has. It has only *one* side—they just drew a continuous line on that one side. How many edges does it have? Again only one. If they don't believe you, have them trace an edge, starting anywhere and follow it with their finger. They will wind up at the exact point they started.

Now this thing just gets more and more curious. In the middle of the strip, punch the point of a pair of scissors through and begin cutting lengthwise. Ask the students what will happen when you get back to the point of origin and cut through. What kind of figure will they get? Oddly, not two strips but one and if you cut *that* strip lengthwise you get two interlocking strips. A strange little critter to say the least. Refer them to the math teacher who can introduce them to the field of topology. By the way, some astronomers think the universe may be shaped this way and that if you threw a baseball hard enough and waited long enough it would hit you in the back of the head. Is this weird stuff or what?

Day 20

Word of the Day:

chaparral (shap a rel)

A word of the southwestern U.S. describing:

(A.) A thicket of shrubs and small trees (noun)
B. A large ranch
C. A roughly circular corral
D. A pasture for horses and cattle

Use: The horses were tired so we stopped near a *chaparral* and gave them a rest.

Thought of the Day:

"Fanaticism consists of redoubling your efforts when you have forgotten your aim." *Santayana*

Hook:

Technically this is a math manipulative, but don't tell the students that. Just tell them it's magic. Have them:
(1) Pick a lucky number between 1 and 10.
(2) Double it.
(3) Add five.
(4) Multiply that number by 50.
(5) If they've already had a birthday this year, add 1755; if not, add 1754.
(6) Now subtract the four-digit number of the year of their birth.

They now have a three digit number. The first digit is their lucky number, the second two digits are their age. (Note: This is calculated for the year 2005. For the year 2006 change the numbers in step 5 to 1756 and 1755 respectively, and add one to each number for each year thereafter).

Day 21

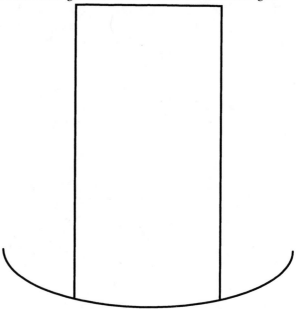

Word of the Day:

sojourn (so´ jurn)

A. The blanket used as padding beneath a saddle
B. A hobo or vagabond
C. A short stay, brief residence (noun)
D. To call a meeting to order

Derivatives: sojourns, sojourned, sojourning, sojourner
Use: We did so enjoy Jim's *sojourn* with us, but alas, all too soon, he had to be moving on.

Thought of the Day:

"A person gazing at the stars is at the mercy of the pebbles in the road." *Anon*

Hook:

Below is the traditional top hat optical illusion. Project it on the screen or simply hold up the sheet for all to see. Ask: "Is the brim wider than the hat is tall? Is the hat taller than it is wide? Or are they the same?" After the students have made their guesses, measure the width and height.

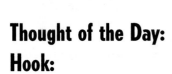

For a full-sized reproducible of this picture, see Appendix, page 209.

Solution:

Surprise! While the brim is actually a bit wider than the hat is tall, most folks perceive the hat as being taller than it is wide. The straight lines appear to be longer than the curved line. The straight lines also define a large area that lends visual weight and illusory length to the vertical lines.

Day 22

Word of the Day:

oscitant (oss´ i tant)

(A.) Inattentive (adj.)
B. In constant motion
C. Disagreeable
D. Modest, shy

Derivatives: oscitancy, oscitance

Use: When the test results were reported, Jamie was sorry she had been so *oscitant* during the class lectures.

Thought of the Day:

"A pessimist is a person who thinks everyone is as nasty as him—and hates them for it." *G. B. Shaw*

Hook:

Rita, Nancy, and Kim are having lunch together. One is blue-eyed, one brown-eyed, and one green-eyed, not necessarily in that order. Rita orders a steak. The brown-eyed woman says, "I'm going to fix spaghetti for my kids tonight, so even though the pasta on the menu looks good, I will have a ham sandwich." The blue-eyed woman says, "I'll stick with my vegetarian diet," and orders a salad. Rita asks Kim, "Do you and your husband ever regret not having children?" Match up names with eye colors.

Solution:

In many cases, drawing a matrix will help to keep track of the information as it is generated. You can approach the solution in a number of ways. Here is one: Let's start with the obvious. We know that Rita had a steak. We know the brown-eyed woman has kids and ordered a ham sandwich. We know the blue-eyed woman ordered a salad. We know that Kim does not have children. These are the givens. Here we go with some indirect inferential reasoning: Since Rita had steak, she cannot be brown-eyed because the brown-eyed woman had a ham sandwich. Rita also cannot be blue-eyed because the blue-eyed woman had a salad. Ergo: Rita must be green-eyed. Kim cannot be brown-eyed because she has no kids and the brown-eyed woman does. Kim also cannot be green-eyed because we just established that Rita is green-eyed. Ergo: Kim must be blue-eyed. Since green and blue are already eliminated, that leaves only brown eyes for Nancy. Plugging our hits and misses into the matrix (draw on the board or project):

Not so tough after all. A simple puzzle like the one above can often be done in your head, but sometimes they will have many variables and several inferences that need to be made and you will find the matrix quite helpful in keeping track of what you know and infer.

Day 23

Word of the Day:

spurious (spur´ ee us)

(A.) False, counterfeit (adj.)
B. Down to earth, folksy
C. Excited
D. Extremely angry, irate

Derivatives: spuriousness, spuriously
Use: His *spurious* testimony was obvious to the jury.

Thought of the Day:

"Endurance is nobler than strength and patience nobler than beauty." *Ruskin*

Hook:

This game is called Black Magic, but there are many variations. The premise of the game is that you conspire with one student before class begins. Then you inform the class that that student is psychic. To prove it, you have that student leave the room. You then have the class pick a target (any object in the room). You call the student back into the room and start pointing to various objects in the room. When you point to non-target objects the student will give a "no" response, but when you finally point to the target object the student will immediately say "Yes, that's the target the class selected." How is he or she doing it?

Solution:

Before class, explain to the *psychic* student the premise of the game and tell him or her to wait until you point to something black. The next object you point to will be the target. You can play one round a day and see how long it takes the class to catch on. You may want to allow them to place restrictions upon you such as, "don't look at the target when the student enters the room" or "don't make eye contact with the *psychic* student." Let them impose a new restriction each day. Then play another round and when the *psychic* picks the target again, challenge them to come up with new restrictions. (Hint: They will often think it has to do with the target being the third or fifth object you point to. Let them determine the number of objects you will point to before you point to the target). If, early on, they want the target to be the first object you point to, try to talk them out of it. "That's too easy" or "Come on now, make it harder than that!" Of course, the system won't work in this instance.

What you are using here is the same system third base coaches use in baseball to pass signals to the batter, an *indicator*. The indicator might be touching the bill of the cap, so the batter pays no attention to the signs until he sees the indicator. Then he knows the next signal he sees is the sign the coach wants him to execute. If the students start passing the indicator to other classes or sections, change the indicator. Now it might be something blue or something metal or a piece of clothing. This will keep them guessing.

26

Day 24

Word of the Day:

occlude (aw clued´)

A. To agree
B. To obstruct (verb)
C. To obscure
D. To exclude

Derivatives: occluded, occluding, occludes, occlusion, occlusive, occludent
Use: I implore you Senator, do not *occlude* the passage of this important legislation.

Thought of the Day:

"There are no mistakes in life, only lessons. As long as you live the lessons will continue." *Anon*

Hook:

Statistics and short anecdotes can give kids a wake-up call about the world in which they live. When your kids begin to assume smugly that the rest of the world is more or less like America, show this to them. This was given to me by a student. I have no idea where he got it, but I have since checked out the numbers and they are reasonably accurate.

If we could, at this moment, shrink the world's population to a village of precisely 100 people, with all existing human ratios remaining the same, that village would look like this:

The village would be made up of:
61 Asians
12 Europeans
14 North and South Americans
13 Africans

70 would be non-white
70 would be non-Christian
6 would control 50% of the entire wealth of the village and they would all be from the U.S.
70 would be unable to read
50 would suffer from malnutrition
80 would live in substandard housing
Only 1 would have a college education

Rather startling, but there are times when we Americans need to realize the world is not very much like us at all. We are the exception, not the rule. No wonder we Americans have such difficulty understanding and appreciating other countries and cultures, and no wonder the rest of the world often regards us as arrogant and out of touch with world reality.

Day 25

Word of the Day:

schlep (shlep)

A. Sleight of hand, stage magic
B. A legal term to indicate responsibility
C. A stupid or clumsy person (noun) (slang)
D. An act, a deception

Use: I felt like a real *schlep* after I dropped and broke my mom's favorite vase.

Thought of the Day:

"Genius without education is like silver still in the mine." *Ben Franklin*

Hook:

Here's a quickie that always astounds. Have a student come to the board. You turn your back. Tell the student to write any number of three or more different digits. Now have the student create a new number by mixing up the same digits that were in the first number. Now have him or her subtract the smaller number from the larger. Announce that the student has now created a new number that you could not possibly know. Have the student circle any single digit in that number except zero. Now tell him or her to tell you only the digits *not* circled. When the student does this, you can immediately tell what number has been circled.

Solution:

It has to do with digital roots. The math teacher can explain it to you, but here's how to do it. When the student tells you what numbers are not circled, mentally add them together. When you get that total, if it is a single digit go directly to the next step. If it is more than a single digit add the digits of the number together to get a new total. If you still have more than one digit, add the digits of that new total to get an answer. Keep doing this until you have a single digit answer. The final step is to subtract that single digit number from nine and *presto*, that is the number the student circled. If the single digit number is nine, then nine is the circled number. Below is an example:

Student chose: 63521
New number: 16253
Subtract: 47268
Circled: 6
Not circled: 4+7+2+8 = 21
Add digits: 2+1 = 3
Subtract from 9: 9-3 = 6

Day 26

Word of the Day:

pernicious (per nish´ us)

A. Nitpicking
B. Dangerous, deadly (adj.)
C. Headstrong, stubborn
D. Lazy

Derivatives: perniciousness, perniciously
Use: It was tragic that Mary became involved with him before she knew of his *pernicious* nature.

Thought of the Day:

"To stretch your mind and broaden your horizons it is necessary to experience intellectual discomfort." *Steve Young*

Hook:

The King has 10 bags of coins. Nine of the bags contain genuine coins, each coin weighing 1 ounce. One bag, however, contains fake coins, each weighing ½ ounce. The royal scales are old and creaky and, in fact, will break after only one more weighing. The King wants you to determine, in only one weighing, which bag contains the counterfeit coins. How do you do it? (A weighing consists of placing x number of coins on the scale and reading that weight—you may not add or subtract coins from those on the scale.)

Solution:

Label the bags 1–10. Place one coin from bag number one in a sack, two coins from bag number two into the same sack, three coins from bag number three, and so forth until you have placed a progressive number of coins from each bag into the sack. You now have 55 coins in the sack. Now weigh the sack. If all coins were genuine the weight would be 55 ounces, but if the weight is 54 ½ ounces that means the sack is ½ ounce light. There is one fake coin in the weighed sack and it must have come from bag number one because if the fake coins had come from bag number two, the weight would be 54 ounces—1 ounce too light (½ plus ½). If the fake coins came from bag number three, the weight would be 53 ½ ounces (½ plus ½ plus ½), and so forth.

Day 27

Word of the Day:

vociferous (vo sif´ er us)

(A.) Loud and vehement (adj.)
B. Covered with sores
C. Pertaining to evil and/or the devil
D. Eternal, without end

Derivatives: vociferously, vociferousness
Use: Hearing Bill's *vociferous* support for the plan, I decided to examine it again before voting.

Thought of the Day:

"There are no ugly women—but only women who have not yet discovered how to reveal their beauty." *Anon*

Hook:

Now here's one that not only requires a little deductive logic, but some knowledge of science as well. (This would be a good one to introduce in class and give them some time to research in order to find the solution.) A lifelong resident of a small remote village receives a mysterious note telling him to row to the middle of a nearby lake at midnight tonight or face public humiliation. He has led a relatively righteous life, but is intrigued by the note and the challenge. So, as midnight approaches, he travels to the lake, gets into a small rowboat, and rows to the middle of the lake. He checks his watch. It is 12:02 a.m. He listens to the ripples in the lake as the wind blows the bow of the boat around slightly and notices the reflection on the water of the small sliver of the crescent moon, high in the sky, as the wind lays. He suddenly hears a sound, begins to turn, and screams. The next morning his lifeless body is found floating in the lake. The question: Did this man vote for Harry Truman in the presidential election of 1948? (No, that's not a typo, and, yes, it can be answered with the information given).

Solution:

The answer is no. The key is the sliver of the crescent moon that was visible at midnight. This condition only occurs in the extreme northern latitudes. Although Alaska is a possibility, Alaska did not join the union until 1959. The man therefore could not have been a citizen of the United States in 1948 and ergo, could not have voted in that election.

Day 28

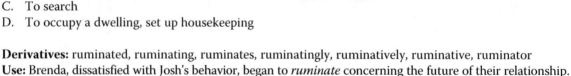

Word of the Day:

ruminate (ru´ mi nate) (long a, silent e)

(A.) To meditate, muse (verb)
B. Leftover, remainder
C. To search
D. To occupy a dwelling, set up housekeeping

Derivatives: ruminated, ruminating, ruminates, ruminatingly, ruminatively, ruminative, ruminator
Use: Brenda, dissatisfied with Josh's behavior, began to *ruminate* concerning the future of their relationship.

Thought of the Day:

"The most common sort of lie is that by which we deceive ourselves. The deception of others is, by comparison, a rare offense." *Nietzsche*

Hook:

A man discovered the grandfather clock in his house had run down so he did not know the correct time. He had no other timepieces with which to reset it correctly. He left his house, walked to a friend's house about a mile away, played a game of chess, then returned home by the same route and used the same pace as before. He took no timepiece with him from his friend's house. When he got home he was able to correctly set his grandfather clock. How did he do it?

Solution:

Even though he didn't know the time, he wound his grandfather's clock and set it to an arbitrary time (let us say he set it to 4:00). He then walked to his friend's house whereupon he noted the time upon entering the friend's house from a clock on the wall (let us say it was 8:00). He then played the game of chess and checked the time again just before leaving (let us say it was now 10:00). He now knows he has played chess for 2 hours. He walks home and checks his grandfather clock immediately upon entering his own house (let us say it now reads 7:00). He now knows he has been away for a total of 3 hours. Since he played chess for 2 hours, his travel time to and from the friend's house was 1 hour (3 hours total minus the 2 hours of chess time). Divide the 1 hour travel time in half and he walked 30 minutes each way to and from his friend's house. Since it was 10:00 when he left the friend's house and his travel time was 30 minutes, this means he arrived back home at 10:30 and he could correctly set his clock.

Day 29

Word of the Day:

trenchant (tren chant)

A. A digging tool
B. A trench dug in a zigzag path
C. Without remorse
D. Incisive, forceful (adj.)

Derivatives: trenchancy, trenchantly
Use: His *trenchant* comments were very persuasive.

Thought of the Day:

"If common sense is so common, why do so few use it?" *Anon*

Hook:

Here's a conundrum for them: You are standing in a room without windows, with a red ball in your hand. You reach over to the wall switch and turn off the lights. The room is now in total darkness. What color is the ball now?

Solution:

When the room is in total darkness, the ball has no color at all. Remember, color is contained in light, not the object. Is it then black, which is defined as the absence of reflected light? Is black really a color? Welcome to the world of hair splitting.

Day30

Word of the Day:

kibitzer (kib´ it zur)

A. A cook or chef
B. An onlooker who offers advice (noun)
C. A tube or bearing that rotates inside a sleeve
D. A German artillery piece of World War I

Derivatives: kibitzed, kibitzing, kibitzes
Use: Fred wasn't very good at chess, so instead of playing, he settled for becoming an unwelcome *kibitzer*.

Thought of the Day:
Hook:

"Don't be humble. You're not that great." *Golda Meir*

This paradox is attributed to Henry Ernest Dudeney. There are three houses that stand next to each other. There are three utility companies (gas, water, and electricity) that stand ready to provide their services to the houses.

The problem is that the owners of the houses want each utility delivered to their houses as separate, direct lines from the utility plants, but they don't want the lines to cross in any manner whatsoever. Can you do it?

For a full-size reproducible of this image, see Appendix, page 210.

Solution:

Sorry. Now it says *separate* lines, so that rules out running one line inside another, and since they can't cross in *any manner whatsoever*, that rules out running one under or over the other. Since each line has to be delivered *directly from utility plant to house*, that rules out going in one side of a house and out the other. Conclusion: insolvable.

Day31

Word of the Day:

rebarbative (ree bar´ ba tiv)

A. Argumentative
B. Ugly, repellent (adj.)
C. Incorrect, mistaken
D. After the fact

Use: Not only was the music much too loud, we also found the repeated use of discords to be *rebarbative.*

Thought of the Day:

"The secret of happiness is not to be found in seeking more, but rather in developing the capacity to enjoy less." *Dan Millman*

Hook:

Here is another of those intriguing questions. You look up on a starry night and happen to see a particular star in the sky. It so happens that this star is so far away (a thousand light years) that its light does not reach earth for 1,000 years. Suppose that one year ago the star went supernova and no longer exists. What are you seeing? Are you actually seeing something that no longer exists? If we could travel to a faraway planet near where that star used to exist and begin looking at earth through an unbelievably powerful telescope, could we actually see events that occurred 1,000 years ago? If we traveled only halfway to the former location of the star, would we see 500 years into earth's past? Would this, in a way, be a time machine? By traveling a specified part of the way to that distant planet, could we not zero in on a particular day and time in earth's history, at least within the last thousand years? (Do I hear the *Twilight Zone* theme?)

Day 32

Word of the Day:

a priori (ah´ pree or´ ee)

A Latin phrase meaning:

A. Unable to reach a decision
B. Inedible
C. Based on untested assumptions or theory (adj.)
D. Existing only in the mind

Use: Since we have been unable to test the prototype, any conclusions we make at this time will have to be *a priori.*

Thought of the Day:

"Life is like a candle, a splendid torch to be made to burn as brightly as possible before passing it on to future generations." *G. B. Shaw*

Hook:

This one is called *Topsy Turvy* or *Bottoms Up*. You will need three cups. Paper cups are easiest, but you can use drinking glasses as well. Position the three cups as illustrated with the cups on each end mouth up and the cup in the middle mouth down.

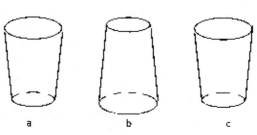

Tell the students you are going to make only three moves and that at the end of the third move all three glasses will have their bottoms up. Do this quickly and do it only once:

Move 1: invert cups b and c
Move 2: invert cups a and c
Move 3: invert cups b and c

Now all three cups do indeed have their bottoms up. Invert cup b and challenge a student to repeat the trick. He or she will be unable to, because when you inverted cup b, it appeared that everything was as before. It is not, so the student will be unable to achieve bottoms up.

Day 33

Word of the Day:

obsequious (ob see´ quee us)

A. Quarrelsome
B. Complicated, complex
C. Habitually late
D. Submissive, obedient (adj.)

Derivatives: obsequiously, obsequiousness
Use: If Susan would just stop being so *obsequious* and start standing up for her own ideas, people might take her more seriously.

Thought of the Day:

"When you want to get absolutely nothing useful accomplished, committees quickly become indispensable." *Anon*

Hook:

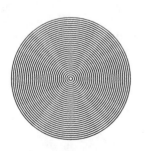

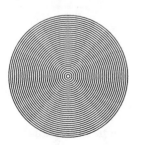

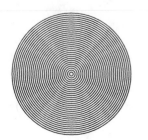

Moires are fun. It would take a physicist most of the afternoon to explain how moires work. Suffice it to say that when you take some patterns and overlay them with other patterns you sometimes get very unusual results. For example, take the series of concentric circles found at the left.

Now comes the fun. Duplicate these on an overhead transparency. Then cut them out so you have three separate sets of circles. Now, on the projector, overlay them and see what happens. Move them around on each other. Neat, huh?

It's a lot of fun to try different patterns and then, instead of simply repeating the same pattern, try overlaying different patterns on each other. You can also duplicate them in different colors for even more unique effects.

While we are on moires, here's something else to try. Scan the three circles onto your computer screen. Now shrink them about 10% at a time and watch the moires begin to show up without even overlaying anything. What you are seeing is the scanning lines of your monitor creating moires as they interact with the circle patterns. Typically the more you reduce, the more pronounced the moire effect, at least to a point. Let your students bring in other designs to try.

For a full-size reproducible of this image, see Appendix, page 211.

Day 34

Word of the Day:

tureen (tu reen´)

(A.) A deep, covered bowl (noun)
B. A dark blue-green color
C. A short, light-hearted musical composition
D. A turncoat, traitor

Use: When David suddenly arose from the dinner table, jerking the tablecloth, the *tureen* went bounding across the floor, Irish stew soaking everything in sight.

Thought of the Day:

"While forbidden fruit is said to taste sweeter—it also usually spoils faster."
Abigail Van Buren

Hook:

A toughie: You are on an island on which there are two tribes of natives. The Quombas always tell the truth and the Zatoffs always lie. While walking toward the nearby village of Lotsaluck, you come to an unmarked fork in the road. You do not know which fork is the correct one to take to the village. Now for some good news and some bad news. The good news is that there is a native standing beside the road who knows the way to the village. The bad news is that you don't know from which tribe he comes and you may ask him only *one* question to determine which is the correct fork to take to the village. What question do you ask?

Solution:

Point to one of the forks and ask, "If I asked a member of the *other* tribe if this is the correct way to Lotsaluck, what would he say?"

There are four possibilities:
1. I am pointing to the *correct* fork and asking a Zatoff.
2. I am pointing to the *correct* fork and asking a Quomba.
3. I am pointing to the *wrong* fork and asking a Zatoff.
4. I am pointing to the *wrong* fork and asking a Quomba.

In case number one, the Zatoff would know that a Quomba would tell the truth and say yes, so the Zatoff would lie and say "no."
In case number two, the Quomba would know that the Zatoff would lie and say no, so the Quomba would tell the truth and say "no."
In case number three, the Zatoff would know the Quomba would tell the truth and say no, so the Zatoff would lie and say "yes."
In case number four, the Quomba would know the Zatoff would lie and say yes, so the Quomba would tell the truth and say "yes."
Logic would dictate that if the answer is "no," it must be the correct fork. If the answer is "yes," it must be the wrong fork.

Day 35

Word of the Day:

lexicon (lex´ i con)

A.   A clear polymer used in car windshields
B.   A written musical composition in a major key
C.   A dictionary (noun)
D.   A major disaster

Use: If you don't know the meaning of the word, you might try looking it up in the *lexicon*.

Thought of the Day:

"Most people tend to drive headlong into the future with their eyes on the rearview mirror." *Marshall McLuhan*

Hook:

In a single elimination tournament in which there are 291 teams competing, how many games must be played to determine the winner?

Solution:

290. This requires no math. Look at it this way: For one team to win, 290 teams have to lose. The championship game will yield both the 290th loser and the winner.

A Follow Up:

Suppose that tournament was *double* elimination. Does the answer change? Is there a *single* answer?

Solution:

580 if the champs remained undefeated (290 teams have to lose twice) and 581 if the champs lost one game.

Day 36

Word of the Day:

transient (trans´ e ent)

A.   A traveler
B.   The bearer of a message
C.   Temporary (adj.)
D.   Moving, in motion

Derivatives: transiently, transientness, transience
Use: Luckily the sunspot interference was of only a *transient* nature and TV reception was quickly restored.

Thought of the Day:

"Those whose thoughts, feelings, and actions have changed—whose discontent is with imperfections in themselves as well as those of the world, have been touched by a teacher." *Anon*

Hook:

Consider this statement: *This statement is false.* Why is this a paradox? Can the paradox be resolved?

Solution:

It's a paradox all right. If the statement is true, then the statement is false, which makes it true, which makes it false, which . . . ad infinitum, ad absurdum. Self contradictory, the statement is a true and unresolvable paradox.

Day 37

Word of the Day:

ninny (nin´ ee)

A. A female donkey
B. A small decorative porcelain figure
C. A fool (noun)
D. A sudden shiver

Use: Start using your head and stop acting like a *ninny*.

Thought of the Day:

"Just because the plumbing works doesn't mean you should drain the tank."
Steve Young

Hook:

Announce to the class that you know they have a secret country where they would like to hide and escape taking your examinations. But tell them what a great detective you are and even though they are going to hide and try to confuse you, you will be able to find in which country they are hiding.

Prepare the graphic below as a poster, overhead transparency, computer graphic, or just write the countries on the board in large letters so the entire class can easily see.

**EGYPT FRANCE GERMANY JAPAN ESTONIA
AUSTRALIA ARGENTINA GREECE
KOREA PERU SPAIN CHINA VIETNAM NORWAY**

Tell the class to select the first stop on their way to their secret country (in other words, pick a country from the list, but don't tell anyone which country they have selected).

Next, show them cards similar to the ones above (these need to be large enough for all to see and remember, as they will have something printed on the back).

Tell the students to select a card that shows a letter in the name of the country they selected. If the country has two or more letters, they have a choice (in other words, if "Vietnam" was the country they selected, they could choose either the letter A *or* the letter E). Tell them to concentrate on that card as you turn the cards over to reveal the back.

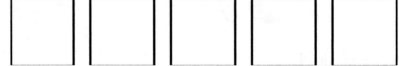

(Remember: Belgium is printed on the back side of A, Thailand is printed on the back side of B, etc.). Remind the students as you go along that they picked the original country, they picked the letter, and now they are resting on a country that you cannot possibly know. Now tell them to move one card (country) over from the country on which they now rest. If they are on either end, they have only one direction to move, but if they are in the middle, they may move in either direction they wish (e.g., if they were resting on Belgium, they must move to Thailand, but if they were resting on Thailand, they may move to either Sweden *or* Belgium). Now have them move again, one card in either direction. Then have them move a third time. Tell them to be sure and remember on which country they are now resting.

You now look over the cards and announce that although Belgium is a good place to hide you know that your students are not there. Now remove the Belgium card and place it aside. Now have the students move one card or country over just as they did moments ago. Have them move a second time, emphasizing they may move in either direction. Then have them move a third time. Again look at the cards and this time announce that although Asia is a great hiding place you know they are not there and *remove* the Thailand card and set it aside. Now tell them they have one final chance to confuse you. Tell them to move one final time in either direction and remember in which country they are hiding. Now dramatically look over the cards and announce that Sweden is not a good hiding place and neither is New Zealand. Removing those cards leaves Scotland as their hiding place. If they have made the moves as you directed, you will be correct. You may want to play additional rounds until they catch on.

Solution:

Examine the first list of countries carefully. While there are plenty of As, Cs, and Es contained in the names, there are no Bs or Ds. This means that when you flip the cards over, they have to be resting on either Belgium, Sweden, or New Zealand. Now, if you move three times from *any* one of those locations, you *cannot* end up on Belgium (so you know they are not there and remove the card). By the way, they also *cannot* end up in Sweden either, which means that when they now move three more times, they *cannot* end up in Thailand (so you remove that card). They also *cannot* be in Scotland, which means that despite whether they are in Sweden or New Zealand, they must move to Scotland as their final move.

Day 38

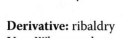

Word of the Day:

ribald (rib´ ald)

A. A European children's game
B. Lewd, vulgar (adj.)
C. Mince pie
D. A holiday celebration

Derivative: ribaldry

Use: Whatever humor the *ribald* ballads may have had was overshadowed by the vulgarities and lewdness of the lyrics.

Thought of the Day:

"The helpless do not revolt, for revolution is an act of hope." *Kropotkin*

Hook:

The teller stole the money from the bank. The question is: Who is the teller? We know the following: Jonathan, Winston, and Pierce work at the bank. One is the manager, one is the cashier, and the other is the teller, but not necessarily in that order. The teller, who is an only child, earns the least. Pierce, who married Jonathan's sister, earns more than the manager. Who's guilty?

Solution:

Winston. Since Pierce earns more than the manager and the teller earns the least, Pierce must be the cashier. Jonathan has a sister and the teller is an only child, making Jonathan the manager. Ergo: Winston is the teller.

Day 39

Word of the Day:

profundity (pro fun´ di tee)

A. A humorous story
B. Depth of meaning or intellect (noun)
C. Confusion
D. A tragic mistake

Derivative: profundities
Use: Bob, normally the class clown, surprised us all with the *profundity* of his poetry.

Thought of the Day:

"A happy man marries the girl he loves, but a happier man loves the girl he marries." *Anon*

Hook:

The boss indicates to the secretary that she needs a document word processed. The secretary indicates that there is a lot of work to do and asks if he can type the document over the next few days averaging 20 pages per day. The boss okays that plan. However, after a few days the secretary comes back to the boss and explains, "there was so much other work to do, I have only been able to average 10 pages per day and the document is only half done. Suppose for the remainder of the document I average 30 pages per day? Half of the document processed at 10 pages per day and half of the document processed at 30 pages per day should average out to 20 pages per day." If you were the boss would this be acceptable?

Solution:

Sounds reasonable, but in reality what the secretary has suggested is impossible. Let us assume the document is 100 pages long. Processing half the document at 10 pages per day would mean 50 pages processed in 5 days. But wait! If the secretary wants to average 20 pages per day, that would mean the total of 100 pages would have to be processed in 5 days. He has already used 5 days in processing the first half of the document, so to arrive at an average of 20 pages per day, *he would have to process the second half of the document in no time at all!*

Day 40

Word of the Day:

stalwart (stal´ wert)

A.   A barrier built to withstand an enemy barrage
B.   A healing herb
C.   Lazy, shiftless
D.   Physically and morally strong (adj.)

Derivatives: stalwartly, stalwartness
Use: Steadfastly refusing to compromise his principles, David, ever *stalwart*, stood convincingly before us.

Thought of the Day:

"Lack of confidence is not the result of difficulty. The difficulty comes from a lack of confidence." *Seneca*

Hook:

Here's an easy card trick that will confound students: Before class, take out the four Jacks and any other three cards from the deck. Fan the four Jacks as shown at left, hiding the other three cards behind the Jacks so that they cannot be seen. Set aside.

When the students are seated, hand the deck, minus the seven cards, to a student. Tell that student to verify that you have not hidden an extra set of Jacks in the deck. While he or she is doing that, pick up the Jacks, making sure you hold and present them in such a way as to keep the three cards behind hidden. Now for the patter: "You know, not many people know that the Jacks are really very good buddies. They hate to be kept apart. In fact, no matter how hard you try to separate them, they always find their way back together again." Have the student place the deck on his or her desk or a table. Now close the fan so that you have the four jacks facing the students with the three cards behind them. Quickly place the seven cards (students think there are four) face down on the other cards of the deck. The three hidden cards will now be the top cards with the Jacks under them. Tilt the deck downward slightly so there is no chance the students will see the faces of the cards. Take the top card (one of the hidden cards that the students think is a Jack) and bury it at the bottom of the deck. Take the second hidden card and bury it about halfway in the deck. Then take the third hidden card and bury it about a third of the way down. Now take the next card (a Jack) and show it to the students telling them it is the fourth Jack. Place it face down back on the deck. Say, "We have now separated the four Jacks, but you know you just can't keep friends apart." Now pull off the top card and show it. They know it's a Jack. But they will be surprised when the next card is a Jack and the next and the next!

Day 41

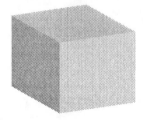

Word of the Day:

tawdry (taw´ dree)

A. Light brown
B. A factory where leather is processed
C. Out of date, obsolete
D. Cheap or gaudy (adj.)

Derivatives: tawdrily, tawdriness
Use: Her excessive makeup and use of gaudy costume jewelry could only be characterized as *tawdry*.

Thought of the Day:

"There is more to life than increasing its speed." *Mahatma Gandhi*

Hook:

There are three sealed boxes. The first box is labeled *gizmos*, the second box is labeled *thingamabobs*, and the third box is labeled *gizmos and thingamabobs*. You are told that each of the three boxes is labeled *incorrectly*. You may open only one box and withdraw only one article from that box. You are then to correctly label each of the three boxes. How do you do it?

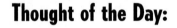

Solution:

Make your selection from the box labeled *gizmos and thingamabobs.* Since that box does not contain a mixture (because it is mislabeled), whatever object you pull from the box will identify what is in that box (whether it be gizmos or thingamabobs). You now have that box correctly identified and you simply switch the other two labels, giving you all three boxes correctly labeled.

Day 42

Word of the Day:

pecuniary (pee qu´ nee air ee)

A. Nitpicking, fault finding
B. Strange, unusual
C. Pertaining to money or finances (adj.)
D. A bird sanctuary

Use: We had to make *pecuniary* arrangements to cover our financial losses.

Thought of the Day:

"Tact consists of knowing how far to go too far." *Jean Cocteau*

Hook:

Here is a variation of an old parlor game that I have adapted for the classroom. You can read the instructions or distribute them via a handout. The premise is simple and once the students learn the game, a round can be played quickly. I used the game both as an occasional hook and sometimes as a reward. Students don't know that they are actually learning deductive reasoning!

Twenty Questions

"Twenty Questions" is a deductive guessing game. The better you are at constructing questions that can narrow down the possibilities, the more likely you are to win. The game may be played by as few as two people, but is a lot of fun to play in teams. To introduce the game, the teacher will provide the target and the class will be divided into teams of three or four students each.

Rules: The first team to correctly identify the target wins the round. The teacher chooses a target. The target must be a noun and must fit into one of three categories: *animal*, *vegetable*, or *mineral*. These are defined as follows:

Animal: Any living or once-living creature (nonplant), either fictitious or real. It may be a specific animal like *Mother Theresa*, or a classification of animal life like *Tennessee Walking Horses*.

Vegetable: Any form of living or once living plant life (not confined to edible plants from the garden). It may be fictitious or real, a specific plant form like *Scotch Pine Tree*, or a general classification of plants like *shrubs*.

Mineral: Any substance, place, or thing that is nonliving (not confined to ore deposits from the ground). It may be real or fictitious, natural or human-made, and specific like *The Lincoln Memorial* or a general classification like *submarines*.

The teacher announces whether the target is animal, vegetable, or mineral. Each team now composes a question. The question must be able to be answered by a *Yes* or *No*. The question is written on a piece of paper and numbered. The group then motions to the teacher that the question is ready. The teacher will walk from group to group, pausing to silently read and then answer that question. As soon as the first question is answered, the group composes its next question, writes and numbers it, and awaits the teacher's answer. Each group may ask only one question at a time. The teacher must then answer the question of at least one other group before returning to the same group. Since each group is competing with the other groups, it will be wise to discuss its choice of questions quietly so as to avoid giving away its strategy.

At any time a team feels sure it knows the answer, its deduction is written on the paper and the team yells "*conclusion.*" All other questioning stops while the teacher checks the answer. A *correct* answer wins the round and the team then briefly explains its reasoning strategy to the rest of the class (and perhaps gloats a bit). An *incorrect* answer disqualifies that team as the winner, but *all* groups continue with the questioning and the disqualified team may still *block* other teams from winning by still being the first group to deduce the answer—in which case there is no winner for that round.

A team that uses all 20 of its questions and is still unable to identify the target (the 20th question must be a conclusion) is disqualified from that round. If no team deduces the answer, there is no winner for that round and the teacher announces the target to the class.

Once the students learn the game format, the rounds will go quickly, but you can speed up the game even more by announcing limits to your target at the beginning. For instance, if you teach history, instead of an animal, vegetable, or mineral, you might declare the target is a famous invention; in music, a type of jazz; in art, a famous artist; in English, a famous novel, etc. By narrowing the limits at the beginning, you can make the game play faster *and* relate it to your own subject. Many variations are possible. After playing under the rules described, you may wish to experiment with your own variations.

Day 43

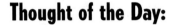

Word of the Day:

kow tow (cow´ taow)

A.   A throw in judo
B.   A parable
C.   To bow or submit (noun)
D.   A Native American tool for skinning animals

Derivatives: kowtowed, kowtowing, kowtows
Use: Since you do everything he wants, you may as well *kow tow* as well.

Thought of the Day:

"One of the hardest things in life to learn is which bridges to burn and which to cross." *Anon*

Hook:

Here is a slightly different type of rebus involving numbers as well as letters. The letters represent words that begin with that letter. Example: 26 L of the A decodes as 26 letters of the alphabet. Now here are three quickies for your students to decode.

1. 9 P of the SS

2. 3 S and YO

3. 30 DHS, A, J, and N

Solution:

1. Nine planets of the solar system

2. Three strikes and you're out

3. Thirty days hath September, April, June, and November

Day 44

Word of the Day:

oleander (o´ lee an der)

- Ⓐ A poisonous evergreen shrub with fragrant flowers (noun)
- B.   A light lubricating oil
- C.   A quilting pattern of stars and star bursts
- D.   A light frivolous mood

Use: The sweet fragrance of *oleander* came wafting from the lovely bouquet.

Thought of the Day:

"When a man murders a tiger, we call it sport. When the tiger murders a man, we call it savagery." *G. B. Shaw*

Hook:

Draw or project the equilateral triangle below. Challenge your students to divide the triangle into three equal areas, each of identical shape.

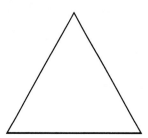

Solution:

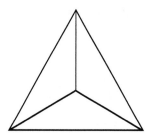

Day 45

Word of the Day:

gauntlet (gont´ let) (also spelled gantlet)

A. The middle mast of a three masted schooner
B. An ornate candlestick
C. A wooden drinking cup
D. A severe trial or challenge (noun)

Use: Alice threw down the *gauntlet* when she told me she could beat me at chess.

Thought of the Day:

"He/she is not the best of statesmen who is the greatest doer, but rather he/she who sets others to doing with the greatest success." *Anon*

Hook:

Inspector Davi had been enjoying the cruise along with the other passengers and was just as surprised when the ship's lookout sighted a single man in a life raft, adrift under a blazing sun. When rescued, he related what had happened as he grabbed a plate of food and began eating voraciously.

"Our ship was the *Mary Lou*, a 26-footer. It went down in a heavy gale. The other four crew members were lost in the storm. I survived in that life raft for five days without any food or water," he said, rubbing the growth of beard on his face. "I guess I could use a shave."

"Are you an experienced sailor?" asked Inspector Davi.

"Oh, yes, I've been a sailor for 20 years," replied the rescued man, wiping some dirty sweat from his brow.

"He's lying. You should hold this man for further questioning," Inspector Davi suggested to the captain.

What *four* things have made the inspector suspicious?

Solution:

1. A vessel only 26 feet in length and small enough to have a crew of only five would be referred to by an experienced sailor as a boat, not a ship.
2. An experienced sailor would refer to his vessel as she or her, not it.
3. A man at sea without food or water for five days would first reach for water, not food.
4. A man at sea for five days, under a hot sun, without water, would be so dehydrated he would not be sweating.

Day 46

Word of the Day:

ennui (awn wee´)

A. Childlike
B. Smiling
C. Enthusiasm
D. Boredom (noun)

Use: The overly long and uninteresting speeches filled us with *ennui*.

Thought of the Day:

"Fear is a darkroom in which negatives are developed." *Neal Wheeler*

Hook:

Project this optical illusion. Are the two vertical lines parallel?

For a full-size reproducible of this image, see Appendix, page 212.

Solution:

Yes, they are, although they seem to diverge slightly at the top. The slanted lines are the culprits, making the vertical lines appear to be farther apart at the top. (Of course, the kids will want you to measure the distance between them to prove it.)

Day 47

Word of the Day:

incognito (in cog neet´ o) also (in cog´ ni tow)

A. In disguise (adj.)
B. Unknown
C. Truthful
D. Free flowing, without disruption

Use: I am on a secret mission and don't want my identity revealed, so I'm traveling *incognito*.

Thought of the Day:

"It's not true that nice guys finish last. Nice guys are winners before the game even starts." *Addison Walker*

Hook:

You have eight balls, all identical in appearance. Seven of the balls weigh precisely the same, but one ball is slightly heavier than the other seven. You have a balance beam. Find the heavy ball in only *two* weighings on the balance beam. (Sure, anyone can do it in three.)

Solution:

Four on a side, two on a side, and one on a side as the first weighing will each produce a situation in which the heavy ball cannot be discerned in one more weighing. But three on each side, with the other two left off the beam will create the following situation: If the beam balances, the heavy ball must be one of the two that were left off. One more weighing will easily find it. If one side drops, the heavy ball must be one of those three so we can eliminate the three balls on the other side of the beam and the two balls left off the beam. We now have three balls left as possibilities. Place a ball on each end of the balance beam, leaving one ball off. If the two balls balance, the heavy ball is the one left off, but if one side drops you have found the heavy ball.

Day 48

Word of the Day:

junta (hoon´ ta)

- A. An English long-throated trumpet used to assemble a fox hunt
- B. A large unleavened cake of Mexico
- C. Military officers who have seized political power and now rule a country (noun)
- D. A small burrowing rodent of the American southwest

Use: The junta ruled with an iron hand after forcibly taking control of the government.

Thought of the Day:

"Be wary of the man who urges action in which he himself incurs no risk."
Joaquin Setanti

Hook:

This time you claim to be psychic and tell the students you know what they are thinking even before they think it. To prove it, you produce an envelope that you give to one of the students for safekeeping. Inside you have written, *An orange kangaroo in Denmark.* Pick a different student. Make a show of producing some random thoughts to make it a real test for your *psychic* powers. Have the student do the following (keeping the answers to him- or herself):

1. Pick a number from one to ten.
2. Multiply that number by nine.
3. If the answer is a single digit, keep that number as your answer. If the answer is a two digit number, add those two digits together to get a new number.
4. Subtract five.
5. Now find the corresponding letter of the alphabet for your new number (If your new number is one, then A is the letter, if your new number is two, B is the letter, etc.).
6. Now think of a European country that *begins* with that letter. (If the student has trouble thinking of one, let the others help while your back is turned).
7. Now take the *last* letter of that European country and think of an animal that *begins* with that letter.
8. Now take the *last* letter of that animal and think of a color which *begins* with that letter.

Ask the student to now reveal what color, animal, and country he or she selected. After it has been revealed, have the student holding the envelope open it and tell the class what is written on the paper inside. Lo and behold you have the color, animal, and country correctly written on the paper.

Solution:

If you haven't already, go back and do steps 1–8 above. Chances are you came up with an orange kangaroo in Denmark. Why? You may let your students do the steps over and over until the solution begins to dawn on them. Steps 1, 2, and 3: Take any number from one to ten, multiply it by nine and what do you get? Any number you pick (other than one) when multiplied by nine will give you two digits that, when added together, give nine as the answer. So no matter what number you picked to start with, your answer at the end of step three will always be nine. Step 4: Subtract five and your new number must be four. Step 5: Since the number must be four, the letter must be D. Step 6: How many European countries begin with D? Only one: Denmark. Step 7: How many animals begin with K? Well, you could say Koala or such, but for most folks, kangaroo jumps (yuk yuk) to mind. Step 8: Ocher is a far out possibility, but again, most people will think orange. So, you see, there is nothing magical or psychic at work, but it may take your students a while to discover what's going on.

Day 49

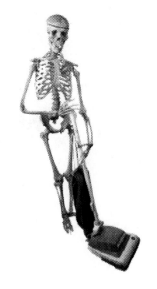

Word of the Day:

insipid (in sip´ id)

A. Bland, without excitement or interest (adj.)
B. Dishonest
C. With great speed or haste
D. Sneaky, sly

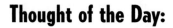

Derivatives: insipidly, insipidness

Use: The movie had such a lame plot, I would have to say it was one of the more *insipid* flicks I have had the displeasure to sit through.

Thought of the Day:

"Action may not always bring happiness, but there can be no happiness without action." *Benjamin Disraeli*

Hook:

Here is yet another type of word puzzle, similar to the rebus. Song titles, movie titles, book titles, and notable quotes have been paraphrased, often using rather stilted vocabulary. The idea is to come up with the original title. (Example: Move hitherward the entire assembly of those who are loyal in their belief = "Oh Come All Ye Faithful"). Here are three quickies:

1. Exited in the accompaniment of an air current typically caused by the interaction of warm and cold air fronts. (Hint: Think Civil War.)

2. A large ebony crow speaking in the eternal negative. (Hint: Think Edgar Allen Poe.)

3. Feudal military men-at-arms assembled at a circular credenza. (Hint: Think Camelot.)

Solution:

1. *Gone With the Wind*

2. Quoth the raven, "nevermore."

3. Knights of the Round Table

Day 50

Word of the Day:

sanctimonious (sank ti mo´ ne us)

- (A.) Pompous, a pretense of righteousness (adj.)
- B. Sacred, consecrated
- C. Pertaining to making difficult decisions
- D. Absolved of responsibility

Derivatives: sanctimoniously, sanctimoniousness, sanctimony
Use: Oh, come on Beth, you don't have to act so *sanctimonious* just because you got that promotion.

Thought of the Day:

"How much more grievous are the consequences of anger than the causes of it." *Marcus Aurelius*

Hook:

Three people, Mr. Clay, Ms. Jones, and Mr. Simms, have different jobs—electrician, plumber, and carpenter. They live in different types of houses—frame, brick, and stone, but not necessarily in the order given. Ms. Jones, who isn't a carpenter, lives in a frame house. Mr. Simms and the person who lives in the brick house live next to each other. The plumber lives in a stone house. Match each person with occupation and type of house.

Solution:

Clay: carpenter, brick house; Jones: electrician, frame house; Simms: plumber, stone house.

Here's one way to figure it. Ms. Jones lives in the frame house (given). Mr. Simms does *not* live in the brick house, ergo: Mr. Simms lives in the stone house, which leaves Mr. Clay living in the brick house. Since the plumber lives in the stone house (given), the plumber has to be Mr. Simms. Ms. Jones is *not* the carpenter, which leaves her as the electrician. That leaves only the carpenter, who has to be Mr. Clay.

Day 51

Word of the Day:

quietus (kwi e´ tus)

A. A state of silence
B. That which suppresses or eliminates (noun)
C. Ornamental buckles on a Spanish saddle
D. The calling to order of a governmental body

Use: The police put the *quietus* on street racing by scheduling more patrols in the area.

Thought of the Day:

"To love and be loved is to feel the sun from both sides." *David Viscott*

Hook:

The king's gold has been stolen. Three unsavories have been rounded up, Dastardly Dan, Slippery Sue, and Hot Fingers Freddy, and we know that one of them is guilty. They make the following statements:

Dan: Sue stole the gold!
Sue: Yes, I stole the gold!
Freddy: Well, I certainly didn't take it!

As luck would have it, we know that at least one of them is lying and at least one of them is telling the truth. Who's lying, who's telling the truth, and who stole the gold?

Solution:

Here's one way to reason it out. If Freddy actually stole the gold, then all three would be lying which we know can't be, ergo: it wasn't Freddy. If Sue stole the gold, then all three are telling the truth, which we know cannot be, ergo: it wasn't Sue, which leaves only Dan. Dan and Sue are lying and Freddy is telling the truth.

Day52

Word of the Day:

insouciance (in so´ see ance)

- (A.) Lack of concern, indifference (noun)
- B. Incapacitation because of liquor or drugs
- C. Unsociability
- D. Anger caused by events beyond one's control

Derivatives: insouciantly, insouciant

Use: His *insouciance* became painfully apparent when he interrupted our interview twice to take cell phone calls.

Thought of the Day:

"It is the customary fate of new truths to begin as heresies and end as superstition." *T. H. Huxley*

Hook:

I call this game *Once Upon a Time* because it involves the student telling a story. Find four unrelated words or phrases, and print them on a card. Now give a student the card and let him or her study it for a few moments. The student will now have one minute to tell a story into which the four target words must be woven, in no particular order. Keep time. If at the end of one minute the student has not woven all four words into the narrative, he or she loses. If, however, the student has succeeded in using the four words, the class (or other team—see below) now has one minute to decide collectively what the four target words were. You can play in teams and keep score if you wish, with one student from team A concocting the story today and a student from team B going next time you play. Award a point for each word the other team did *not* identify as a target word. You, or the students, can even award points for originality of the story itself. When everyone on both sides has had a turn, add up the score and declare a winner. Here is an example you can use to introduce the game to your class:

Target Words: Baseball, Motivated, Albert Einstein, Corvette.

Story: I attended a major league baseball game not long ago. I got to see Ken Griffey Jr. in action. He played a great game, but afterward I spoke with him while he was playing ping pong with some of the other players on his team. He told me that with so many games to play each season, it is sometimes hard to stay motivated. He indicated that while he used to own a Plymouth Fury, the owners of the team had provided some incentive by telling him that if he, or any other member of the team, hit 60 home runs, they would buy that player a new Corvette. He said it didn't take an Albert Einstein to figure out what a great incentive that was. Before I could ask him any other questions, his agent showed up and said he had to make a public appearance at a shopping mall. But he did give me an autographed baseball and a season pass and told me to study hard, especially algebra and history. He told me if I ever get to Cincinnati again, to give him a call, but to be sure and use AT&T because he owns stock in that company. After I came home, I set the ball on the mantle and turned on the TV and watched an old western.

This story is a bit mundane but gets the idea across. Note how I also worked in some *red herrings* that I hoped would mislead the class. Encourage your students to let their imaginations take flight—the more fanciful the story the better. All you need do to prepare for the game is to construct the list of words. Here are a few to get you started:

1. submarine, Christmas tree, curious, wind chimes
2. computer chip, ancient, walking stick, clown
3. calendar, Aspen (Colorado), pogo stick, appreciate
4. flute, convention, insane, Persian rug
5. circus, university, animated, harmful
6. good Samaritan, footstool, foolhardy, monumental
7. Pike's Peak, lemonade, folk song, nickel
8. president, achieve, Old Ironsides, e-mail
9. oak tree, definition, Pacific Ocean, movie star
10. outer space, violin, musty, magnesium
11. evening dress, egg beater, dragon, slippery
12. cup of coffee, handmade quilt, perfume, amazing
13 deck of cards, rosebush, impatient, jet fighter
14. stereo, flower pot, rooster, dismantled
15. snowball, astrological sign, disgruntled, rock 'n' roll
16. limited, rainbow, locomotive, hair dryer
17. head lice, box of matches, laboratory, smiling
18. battleship, mittens, arduous, fountain pen
19. aardvark, illuminated, door handle, New York City
20. crossword puzzle, anchor, disappointed, grass clippings

Day 53

Word of the Day:

bittersweet (bit´ er sweet)

A. A nut of the almond family
B. Nostalgic
C. Deep reddish orange (adj.)
D. Possessing both pain and pleasure (noun)

Use #1: The leaves of the maple, now that it was autumn, were a vivid *bittersweet.*
Use #2: Seeing the woman again who he had loved almost 30 years ago was indeed *bittersweet.*

Thought of the Day:

"The law, in its majestic equality, forbids the rich as well as the poor to beg for bread or sleep under bridges." *Anon*

Hook:

This paradox is attributed to Jules Henri Poincare (1854–1912) and is called the *Nocturnal Doubling Paradox*: What if last night while everyone slept, *everything* in the universe doubled in size? Would there be any way to tell what had happened?

Solution:

Good luck! Remember, all rulers and scales have doubled in size as well. The space between atoms and the atoms themselves would be twice as large, so ratios of mass to size would remain the same. Any ideas?

Day 54

Word of the Day:

flagitious (fla gish´ us)

A. With great pomp and ceremony
B. Weary, dispirited
C. Shockingly brutal or evil (adj.)
D. Advantageous

Derivatives: flagitiously, flagitiousness
Use: The invading army's pillaging of the town was so *flagitious*, it was sickening.

Thought of the Day:

"A well-adjusted person is one who makes the same mistake twice—without getting upset." *Jane Heard*

Hook:

Another rebus:

Y FIREWORKS

Solution:

Fourth of July fireworks (fourth letter of the word July).

Day 55

Word of the Day:

pyrrhic victory (peer´ ik)

A victory that is:

A. Overwhelming
B. So small as not to be considered a victory at all
C. Without bloodshed
D. Won with staggering losses (noun)

Use: Another *pyrrhic victory* such as this and we shall lose the war.

Thought of the Day:

"Love quickens all senses except the common." *Anon*

Hook:

A toughie: There are five people, each of whom is wearing a gold or blue hat. Each can see the hats worn by the other four, but cannot see his or her own hat. Anyone wearing a gold hat always makes true statements. Anyone wearing a blue hat always makes false statements. The following statements are made:

Margo: I see three gold hats and one blue hat.
Earl: I see four blue hats.
Beverly: I see one gold hat and three blue hats.
Joel: (Refuses to say anything.)
Stephanie: I see four gold hats.

What color hat is each person wearing?

Solution:

Although the problem may be solved in a number of different ways, one possible solution follows:

Consider Stephanie's statement. If true, everyone would be wearing a gold hat and they would *all* tell the truth and say, "I see four gold hats." Since they did not, Stephanie's statement is false and she is wearing a blue hat.

Consider Earl's statement. If true, there would be one gold hat (Earl's) and all other statements would be false; but, Beverly's statement would be true that she sees one gold and three blue. This cannot be, so Earl's statement is false and his hat is blue.

We now have positively identified two blue hats, so Margo's statement must be false and she is wearing a blue hat.

Consider Beverly's statement. If her statement is *false*, Joel must be wearing a blue hat, making all five hats blue. If Beverly is lying, then Earl's statement would have to be true and we already know this is not the case. Therefore, Beverly's statement is true, and her hat is gold.

Since Beverly sees one gold hat and three blue hats, Joel's hat must also be gold.

Ergo: Margo, Earl, and Stephanie are wearing blue hats, while Beverly and Joel are wearing gold hats.

Day56

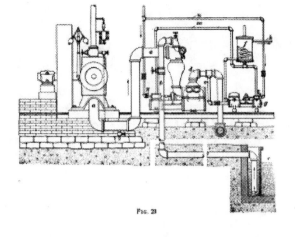

Fig. 23

Word of the Day:

qualm (kwam)

A. The eye of a hurricane
B. A monetary unit of the Czech Republic
C. Doubt or misgiving (noun)
D. Grain raised to be fed to animals

Derivatives: qualmish, qualmishly
Use: I have no *qualms* about implementing the plan immediately.

Thought of the Day:

"Some people need lots of love—others just need a steady supply." *Anon*

Hook:

We all like charades. Give the student the target, which can be the name of a famous person, a movie title, book title, place, or any well-known noun. The student is to act it out *silently* within 1 minute. You can play individually or as a team as discussed earlier. A second target is provided in case you wish to give each team a chance today.

Targets:

(1) Harry Potter
(2) *To Kill a Mockingbird*

Day 57

Word of the Day:

ephemeral (e fim´ er al)

A. Flimsy, sheer
B. Ghostly, eerie
C. Lasting for a short time only (adj.)
D. From a woman's point of view

Derivatives: ephemera, ephemerality, ephemerally
Use: The delicate beauty of the iris is breathtaking but, alas, *ephemeral.*

Thought of the Day:

"Injustice anywhere is a threat to justice everywhere." *Martin Luther King, Jr.*

Hook:

Here's another puzzler. Below are six cards. You may cut them out and use them as cards, scan them into a computer display program, make overhead transparencies, or simply duplicate the sheet and give each student a copy, but you will use the cards one at a time. Have a student pick any number from 1 to 63, but keep it to him- or herself. Tell the student that you will now divine the number. Show the cards to the student(s). Using one card at a time, ask the student if his or her number appears somewhere on the card. When you have gone through the six cards you will miraculously be able to tell the student the number.

For a full-sized reproducible of this image, see Appendix, page 213.

Solution:

On each card the number appears, mentally add the numbers in the upper left hand corner. For example, the student has thought of the number 25. The upper left hand numbers on the cards where 25 appears add up to 25. 1+8+16 = 25. Sequence of using the cards does not matter.

The secret, of course, is that the numbers in the upper left hand corners will *always* add up to the selected number. Note that the numbers 1, 2, 4, 8, 16, and 32 can be added in varying combinations to equal every number from 1 to 63. This one is a real toughie and may take several times before the class catches on.

Day58

Word of the Day:

deference (def´ er ence)

(A.) Polite yielding or submission (noun)
B. Disbelief
C. Without conviction
D. A hearing defect of the inner ear

Derivatives: defer, deferent, deferential, deferentially, deferrer
Use: In *deference* to Lucy's stronger plan, Mike withdrew his own idea for establishing the new park.

Thought of the Day:

"Never insult an alligator until after you have crossed the river." *Cordel Hull*

Hook:

Divide the L shaped figure below into four equal areas, each of identical shape:

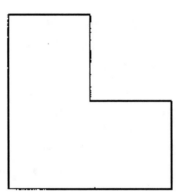

Solution:

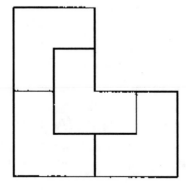

Day 59

Word of the Day:

palatable (pal´ it a bul)

A. Acceptable in taste, agreeable (adj.)
B. Capable of being stacked
C. Friendly, sociable
D. Fast growing

Derivatives: palatability, palatableness, palatably

Use: Chad was about to reject the offer, but when the company threw in a lucrative bonus, it made the deal a lot more *palatable*.

Thought of the Day:
Hook:

"Dreams are true while they last. Can we say more of life?" *Havelock Ellis*

Another bit of humor, which pokes fun at not seeing the forest for the trees.

Sherlock Holmes and Dr. Watson are on a camping trip. They retire for the night. In the early morning hours, Holmes elbows Watson and asks, "Watson look straight up. What do you see?

"Why Holmes, I see a brilliantly starry night."

"And what does that mean to you, Watson?"

"My dear man, it means many things to me," replied the good doctor. "Meteorologically, it means we are in the middle of a high pressure area, the sky is cloudless, rain is nowhere in sight, and we should have another beautiful day for our camping trip."

"And what else does it mean to you?" asked the detective.

"Why, astrologically, it means Mars is in the ascendent. Astronomically, I can see millions of stars from which I can deduce the enormity of our own Milky Way galaxy and the infinite nature of the universe, including the almost certainty of life elsewhere as well as here on our own relatively insignificant sphere."

"Does it mean anything else to you?" asked Holmes.

"Aesthetically, those bright pinpoints of light against the blackness of the sky are absolutely breathtaking, and cosmologically, it gives me pause to wonder at the possibility of a master creator."

Watson pondered a moment then turned to his friend. "And you, Holmes, when you look up and see the stars, what does it mean to you?"

"It means," replied the detective, "that someone has stolen our tent."

Day 60

Word of the Day:

vignette (vin yet´)

(A.) A very brief sketch or description (noun)
B. An herb used to season soups
C. An unpaid debt
D. An orchard, especially a grape orchard

Derivatives: vignetted, vignetting, vignettes
Use: Trish used a *vignette* very effectively to set the stage for the first chapter of her novel.

Thought of the Day:

"Minds of only moderate caliber ordinarily condemn everything which is beyond their understanding." *Anon*

Hook:

Inspector Davi walked up the front walk, past the late model sedan that sat in the gravel driveway, his umbrella shielding him from the drizzle that had been falling since last night.

"Please tell me what happened," he said as the middle-aged man ushered him into the house, and he noticed the body of the dead woman in the living room.

"About an hour ago, my wife screamed that a man was trying to break into our house. I ran to the window just in time to see him pulling away in a gray van. I jumped in our car to follow, but by then he had turned a corner and I lost him. I continued driving for several minutes to try to locate him but it was no use. When I returned home, I found Martha lying here dead from a bullet wound."

"Is the car in the driveway the one you used to chase the man?" asked Inspector Davi.

"Yes it is. I think you'll find the engine is still warm," responded the man.

The inspector walked outside, put his hand on the hood and noticed the warmth. He then opened the hood and noticed a small oil leak dripping from the engine.

"I've been meaning to have that oil leak fixed," said the man, "but it only leaks when the engine warms up and I keep forgetting."

Inspector Davi squatted beside the car and put his hand underneath to feel the patch of oily gravel. Indeed there was warm oil on his fingers when he withdrew his hand.

"Arrest this man! He's lying!" he said to one of the uniformed officers. Why has the inspector come to this conclusion?

Solution:

When he felt the oily gravel under the car, he also felt that the other gravel under the car was *dry*, meaning the car had not left the driveway since last night. The man may have thought to run the engine for a while to support his story, but he forgot to physically move the car.

Day 61

Word of the Day:

marginate (mar´ gi nate)

A. To spread butter or oleo, as on bread
B. To provide with margins or borders (verb)
C. To extinguish, as a candle
D. To use or incorporate an idea that is not mainstream

Derivatives: marginated, marginating, marginates, margination
Use: I really believe your newspaper ad will be more effective if you *marginate* the text using a decorative design.

Thought of the Day:

"Kissing is a means of getting two people so close together that they can't see anything wrong with each other." *Rene Yasenek*

Hook:

Here is an exercise in logic. Given: All Skeetawattas are Cratchets. All Cratchets are hot. Some Cratchets are Packalomers. Some Packalomers are Flateraps. Which of the following conclusions are logical (are accurate deductions based on the information given)?

A. Some Packalomers are hot.
B. Some Flateraps must be Skeetawattas.
C. Some Skeetawattas must be Packalomers.
D. All Skeetawattas are hot.

Solution:

Statements A and D are logical. To illustrate we can use a Venn diagram (sometimes called circles of inclusion/exclusion). The Venn is useful in diagraming alls, somes, and nones.

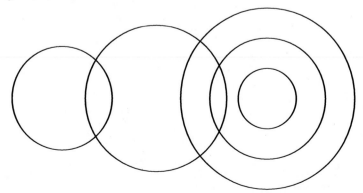

The givens: *All* Skeetawattas are Cratchets is illustrated by the Skeetawattas circle being enclosed entirely within the Cratchets circle. *All* Cratchets are hot is illustrated by the Cratchets circle being enclosed entirely by the hot circle. We would know at this point that *all Skeetawattas are Cratchets and hot* and that *all Cratchets are hot*. *Some* Cratchets are Packalomers is illustrated by the Cratchets circle *partly* intersecting the Packalomers circle. We would also now know that some packalomers are both hot and Cratchets, and that while the Packalomers circle could intersect the Skeetawattas circle, it does not have to. Ergo: Packalomers do not necessarily have to be Skeetawattas and vice versa. *Some* Packalomers are Flateraps is illustrated by the partial intersection of the Packalomers and Flateraps circles. Could the Flateraps also be hot, Cratchets, and even Skeetawattas? Yes, they *could*, but as the diagram shows they don't necessarily have to be.

So, simply looking at the circles it becomes clear that in order for some Cratchets to be Packalomers, those same Packalomers would *have* to be hot. Ergo: A is logical. However, the Flateraps and Skeetawattas circles do not have to touch at all. Ergo: B is not logical. The Skeetawattas circle does not have to touch the Packalomers circle. Ergo: C is not logical. And finally, all Skeetawattas are within the Cratchets circle and all Cratchets are within the hot circle. Ergo: D is logical.

Day 62

Word of the Day:

secular (sek´ u lur)

A. Legal
B. Non-religious in nature (adj.)
C. Partial, incomplete
D. Biased, unfair

Use: The Supreme Court's interpretation of separation of church and state means that all aspects of the government must remain *secular.*

Thought of the Day:

"The life of every one of us is a diary in which we mean to write one story—yet actually write another, and our humblest hour is when we compare the volume as it is with what we vowed to make it." *Barrie*

Hook:

Here's a neat card trick that will amaze. Before class, discard the jokers, and arrange the cards of the deck by suit and by descending order (that is, when face down the ace will be on top, then the king, then the queen, etc.) The suits are stacked on each other in no particular order.

Select a student. Place the deck face down in front of him or her and have the student cut the deck 13 times (No more, no less). The cuts can be made wherever the student wants, but each cut should be a single cut (pick up the partial deck, lay it on the table, and put the remaining cards on top). When the 13th cut has been completed have the student hand you the deck, still face down. As the cards are passed to you, note the bottom card (this can be done while straightening the deck and while you are asking the student to think of a card he or she wants you to find). When the student has a card in mind, give the deck back to him or her, and have the student deal out, in a straight line, face down, 13 cards from the top of the deck (you may need to use a table top). Then have the student repeat the procedure, that is, deal the next 13 cards on top of the 13 just dealt (make sure the cards are dealt from left to right each time). Repeat the procedure twice more until all the cards have been dealt onto the 13 piles.

Now have the student announce to the class which card he or she wants you to find. You will not only be able to find his card, but the other three suits of that card as well, for they will all be together and you know exactly where (as a matter of fact each card in the deck will now be found with the other three matching cards).

Solution:

Here's the secret. When the deck is cut 13 times the cards will automatically arrive back in the same relative position where they started (Yeah, yeah, I know you don't believe it, but just try the trick). That doesn't mean that the ace will necessarily be on top again, but it will be on top of the king which will be on top of the queen, etc.) Since the bottom card, at which you glanced, is now at the far right (on the 13th pile) you know the positions of every card in the deck. Here's how that works: Let's say that you saw that a 10 was on the bottom when the student handed the deck back to you. You know all four 10s are on the 13th pile (the bottom card was the last dealt onto the 13th pile) and since the cards are in descending order that means that the pile on the far left are nines, then the eights, etc.) Let's say the student wants you to find the ace of hearts. You can start at the right and count back (to the left) in ascending order, or count forward (to the right) in descending order. Since you want the aces, count left four spaces and you've found them (see illustration). Now for some patter: "Well, I tell you what, this is a difficult trick, so just to be sure I get your card . . ." Now pick up that pile of four cards, turn them over, and fan them so the students can see, ". . . how about I find all four aces?"

Now place the aces back down and have another student pick another card. Miraculously you will be able to find not just that one card, but all four of that card. You can keep doing this indefinitely until, as your finale, you start from the left and turn over each pile to reveal that all four of a given card are together despite the fact that the student cut the cards and dealt them out.

You may want to practice this at home a couple of times to get used to identifying the bottom card and then counting left or right to find the target cards.

Example illustrated:

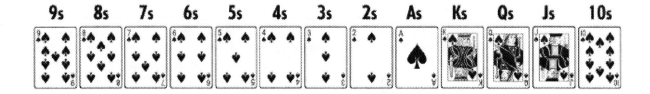

Day 63

Word of the Day:

ostentatious (os ten ta´ shus)

(A.) In a showy, bragging manner (adj.)
B. Generous, giving of oneself
C. Tasty, delicious
D. Famous, well known

Derivatives: ostentation, ostentatiously
Use: Jeff's *ostentatious* display of his new car was in rather poor taste.

Thought of the Day:

"My interest is in the future for it is there I shall spend the rest of my life."
Charles Kettering

Hook:

Here's a logic puzzle that may take a little more time than usual. Perhaps you could allow them to work in teams, have some additional time at the end of the period, or let them take it home and bring back the solution tomorrow.

The baseball team drove home in two cars after the game. The pitcher owned and drove a Chevy, while the Ford was owned and driven by the shortstop. The players were later heard making the following statements:

Bill: I was a passenger in the car in which the third baseman and right fielder were also riding. Our car was blue.

Ben: I rode in the back seat between the catcher and the center fielder. My hometown is Chicago.

Jack: Randy had on a red cap and rode with me and the first baseman.

Art: Steve rode in the Ford. His hobby is playing the guitar.

Phil: Art is an infielder and owns a house in Louisville.

Ozzie: I was in the Ford. The second baseman wanted to stop at a bookstore on the way. The bookstore was on the corner of 2nd and Vine Street.

Steve: We gave a lift to a lady whose Honda had broken down. She had blonde hair and was very pretty. Phil and I sat next to windows. The lady sat between Phil and me, but no one else did.

Randy: I sat next to the pitcher, who isn't married.

Harry: My car carried five of us. We had a flat tire that the player with the blue cap changed. Steve is not the shortstop. Neither is Phil, who doesn't play right field either.

Determine who rode in which car, in which seat, and what position he plays. Bring out the pencil and paper. You will need it to keep track of the information.

Solution:

The Ford contained:

Ozzie: driver, shortstop; Bill: front seat passenger, second base; Phil: rear seat, third base; and Steve: rear seat, right field.

The Chevy contained:

Harry: driver, pitcher; Randy: front seat passenger, left field; Art: rear seat, catcher; Ben: rear seat, first base; and Jack: rear seat, center field. (You, of course, had to disregard several pieces of irrelevant information.)

Day64

Word of the Day:

sabulous (sab´ u lus)

A. Gritty, sandy (adj.)
B. Covered with sores
C. An ornate scabbard for a sword
D. Without regret

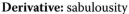

Derivative: sabulousity

Use: We have stirred and stirred, but the mixture, which should be creamy smooth by now, remains *sabulous.*

Thought of the Day:

"Poetry is an echo asking a shadow to dance." *Anon*

Hook:

Here are three more word/number rebuses:

1. N of M in the I 500

2. 7 N of the MS

3. 2 TD and a P in a PT

Solution:

1. Number of miles in the Indianapolis 500

2. 7 notes of the musical scale

3. 2 turtle doves and a partridge in a pear tree

Day 65

Word of the Day:

rapport (ra por´)

(A) A good relationship or bond (noun)
B. A fencing sword of the 19th century
C. Outdated, passé
D. A light meal taken in mid-afternoon

Use: Once he established *rapport* with the natives, the work of the Peace Corps volunteer went smoothly.

Thought of the Day:

"Talk is cheap—because supply always exceeds demand." *Anon*

Hook:

How about a quick exercise in ethics? We have all learned not to lie and we can probably all agree that, as a general rule, we shouldn't lie. Yet, is lying *always* unethical? Consider the following: A married couple, Jim and Sally, your very good friends, are involved in a tragic automobile accident. Jim is killed. Sally, although conscious, is left in critical condition, near death. She does not know the fate of her husband. You have been told that you can see her briefly, but it is of utmost importance that you say nothing to upset her for in her delicate condition bad news could well cause a fatal reaction. As you enter the room, before you can say anything, Sally asks you, "How's Jim?" What do you say?

Solution:

There is no solution per se, but the situation does bring up the issue of so-called *white lies*. What are white lies? What differentiates white lies from other types of lies? What about motive? Is there a difference between lies told for the benefit of the overall good as opposed to those that are self-serving?

Day 66

Word of the Day:

peculate (pek´ u late)

A. To chatter incessantly
B. To dream
C. To steal or embezzle (verb)
D. To complain

Derivatives: peculated, peculates, peculating, peculation, peculator
Use: Luckily, the auditors caught the bookkeeper before he could *peculate* any additional funds.

Thought of the Day:

"Truth is not only violated by falsehood; it may be equally outraged by silence." *Amiel*

Hook:

A woman states that she headed her car north on a straight road and drove for 100 yards. She says she then ended up 100 yards *south* of where she started. She also states there are *two* ways she can do it. Can you figure it out?

Solution:

1. She drove backwards.

2. The front bumper of her car was just shy of the North Pole when she started.

Day 67

Word of the Day:

blasé (bla zay´)

A. A French dessert of chocolate and whipped cream
B. A woman's blouse that has a zipper instead of buttons
C. Bored, jaded, indifferent (adj.)
D. An ascot or any broad, decorative necktie

Use: Joan's *blasé* attitude made it clear she had no real interest in the project.

Thought of the Day:

"One machine may be able to do the work of fifty ordinary people—but no machine can do the work of one extraordinary person." *Edward Hubbard*

Hook:

Seven employees each have a day off each week, no two of them on the same day. Charlotte's day off is the day after Susie's. Charlotte's last vacation ended three weeks ago today. Barbara's day off is three days after the day before Lena's. Lena's lunch period is 30 minutes longer than Luana's. Al's day off is three days before Luana's. Barbara took two sick days last month. Jim's day off is halfway between Al's and Susie's and is on a Thursday. The firm pays double wages for overtime. Which day off does each employee have?

Solution:

There is irrelevant information presented that must be ignored. Charlotte: Sunday; Lena: Monday; Al: Tuesday; Barbara: Wednesday; Jim: Thursday; Luana: Friday; Susie: Saturday.

Day 68

Word of the Day:

jackanapes (jak´ a napes)

A. An impertinent or conceited young man (noun)
B. A hyena from Australia
C. In cards, the jack of spades
D. A small island group off the coast of Chile

Use: Having hidden his character, the *jackanapes* soon revealed his true colors.

Thought of the Day:

"When in doubt, forge ahead. It's almost always easier to get forgiveness than permission." *Anon*

Hook:

A riddle: What occurs once in a second, once in a month, and once in a century, but doesn't occur at all in a week, year, or decade?

Solution:

The letter N.

Day 69

Word of the Day:

ubiquitous (u bik´ qwa tus)

A. Everywhere at once (adj.)
B. Puzzling
C. Convincing
D. Lacking in conviction

Derivatives: ubiquity, ubiquitously, ubiquitousness
Use: Science, in modern society, seems *ubiquitous* in its influence.

Thought of the Day:

"Only the mediocre are always at their best." *Jean Giraudoux*

Hook:

The policeman had a problem. He had captured three mobsters, Lefty, Muggsy, and Bubba, but he now needed to transport them to the police station and there were no other officers available to help. Besides himself, he could transport only one other person at a time. He could make multiple trips, but his quandary was that if he took Bubba, Lefty would shoot Muggsy. If he took Lefty, Muggsy would shoot Bubba. Only when the policeman was present were Muggsy and Bubba safe from their adversaries. Transporting only one suspect at a time, how can he get them all safely to the police station?

Solution:

The policeman takes Muggsy, leaving Bubba and Lefty together. He deposits Muggsy at the station and returns for Bubba, but at the station he leaves Bubba and brings Muggsy back to the point of arrest. He now leaves Muggsy at the starting point and transports Lefty to the station where he leaves him with Bubba. He then returns for Muggsy.

Day 70

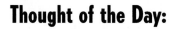

Word of the Day:

tenuous (ten´ u us)

A. Pertaining to muscle tissue
B. Self-satisfied
C. Composed of a metallic alloy
D. Weak, insubstantial (adj.)

Derivatives: tenuously, tenuousness
Use: When the scandal broke, his influence with the electorate became very *tenuous*.

Thought of the Day:

"Tradition is what you resort to when you don't have the time, resources, or imagination to do it right." *Kurt Adler*

Hook:

Here's an inductive thinking activity. The mechanic at the garage states that he works on twice as many Puttputtniks as Belchfires, which he says proves that the Belchfire is a better built automobile. How many arguments can you come up with that could disprove the mechanic's conclusion?

Solution:

Here are a few. Maybe your students will think of more.

1. Maybe the Puttputtnik is a more popular car; therefore, there are a lot more of them on the road, and naturally, more of them would wind up in the shop even though the rate of repair is no worse than the Belchfire.

2. Maybe the garage where the mechanic works specializes in Puttputtniks, so people tend to take their Belchfires elsewhere.

3. Maybe this mechanic is quite good at fixing Puttputtniks and the boss has his other mechanics work on Belchfires.

4. Maybe the Puttputtnik has a better warranty, so Puttputtnik owners are more likely to bring their cars in for repair than Belchfire owners.

5. Maybe the Puttputtniks are brought in more often, but maybe the repairs tend to be less serious than the repairs on Belchfires.

6. Maybe Puttputtnik owners are simply more conscientious about taking care of their cars and bring them in for servicing or minor repairs more often.

Day 71

Word of the Day:

salient (say´ lee ant)

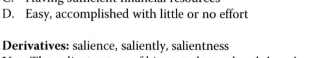

A. Striking or conspicuous (adj.)
B. A type of heat generated by the sun's rays passing through Earth's atmosphere
C. Having sufficient financial resources
D. Easy, accomplished with little or no effort

Derivatives: salience, saliently, salientness
Use: The *salient* nature of his remarks rendered the other arguments moot.

Thought of the Day:

"The young man who has not wept is a savage—and the old man who does not laugh is a fool." *George Santayana*

Hook:

Decode the following paraphrases:

1. Assertive affirmation of self-determination.

2. Omnipotent supreme being who grants respite to jovial cultured males.

3. Maize atop the male Cygnus.

Solution:

1. Declaration of Independence

2. "God Rest Ye Merry Gentlemen"

3. Corn on the cob

Day72

Word of the Day:

garrulous (gaer´ a lus)

A. Happy-go-lucky, carefree
B. Excessively talkative (adj.)
C. Argumentative
D. To act in an immoral manner

Derivatives: garrulously, garrulousness
Use: With his *garrulous* nature, it was hard to get in a word edgewise.

Thought of the Day:

"The only people who achieve much are those who want knowledge so badly they seek it while the conditions are unfavorable. Favorable conditions never happen." *C. S. Lewis*

Hook:

A teacher announces that there will definitely be a test one day next week. She then announces that the test day will come as a complete surprise because there will be no way the students can know beforehand which day it will be.

One student reasons thusly: The test can't come on Friday, because if we get through Thursday without the test being given, then we will know it has to be on Friday. Now considering Thursday: If Friday is already eliminated, we can eliminate Thursday as well, since if we get through Wednesday then we will know it has to be Thursday. As a matter of fact, he reasons, we can eliminate every day next week by using the same reasoning. The teacher simply cannot give the test at all. He shares his reasoning with the other students who rejoice to find out the teacher will be unable to give the test. Imagine their surprise when on Tuesday (or any day you like) the teacher walks in and gives the test.

What was wrong with the student's reasoning?

Solution:

Friday can be eliminated only after Thursday has come and gone with no test. If you got as far as Wednesday with still no test, you cannot, at that point, eliminate Thursday because 2 days still remain as possibilities. The same is true of Wednesday (3 days remaining), Tuesday (4 days remaining) and Monday (5 days remaining). While the student's reasoning *sounds* workable, this is called a priori reasoning, reasoning before the actual situation occurs, which, in this case, is just plain wrong (as the class unfortunately found out).

Day 73

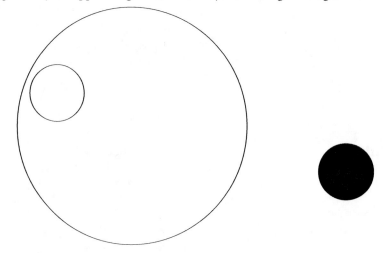

Word of the Day:

pedantic (pe dan´ tik)

(A.) Of formal learning, but no real world experi-
    ence (adj.)
B. An animal lover
C. A bicyclist
D. One who has a fascination for shoes

Derivatives: pedant, pedantical, pedantically

Use: John found his *pedantic* education had to be tempered with real world experiences to be of much practical value.

Thought of the Day:

"Don't be afraid of opposition. Remember, a kite rises against, never with the wind." *Hamilton Mabie*

Hook:

Below is an optical illusion to project or hand out. Which of the two smaller balls is larger, white or black?

Solution:

Both are the same size, although the black ball appears smaller. The reasons are twofold. First, things appear larger against an established field. This is why the moon appears so much larger as it nears the horizon. Secondly, lighter objects appear larger than dark objects on a light background.

For a full-sized reproducible of this image, see Appendix, page 214.

Day 74

Word of the Day:

offal (aw´ ful)

A. Wondrous
B. Left over waste material (noun)
C. Of little value
D. Determined, unstoppable

Use: The *offal* from the strip mine was beginning to pollute the small creek near our home.

Thought of the Day:

"Nature, quite wisely, has given us two ears but only one mouth." *Benjamin Disraeli*

Hook:

Here's a neat demonstration in psychology to try.

Tell the students you want to check the acuity of their hearing. Produce a tape recorder, the fancier the better. Tell your students you are going to play a tape of a high pitched tone. You will start the volume at zero and gradually increase the volume until those students with the most sensitive hearing will finally hear it. When they do, they should raise their hands. You will then keep raising the volume until all students can finally hear it. Make a show of turning on the recorder and gradually turning up the volume control. In reality you are playing back nothing, but the students don't know that. Look expectantly across the room as you continue to turn up the volume. Chances are, at least a couple, if not more, of the students will eventually raise their hands. You will then want to explain, in such a way as not to embarrass those whose hands were raised, that expectation is a very strong psychological force.

Solution:

What they have just experienced is a form of auditory hallucination. When we are expecting company, we will sometimes *hear* a car pulling into the driveway, only to find there is nothing there. Another example is exploring a haunted house. We may think we hear creepy sounds simply because we expect to, or natural sounds (such as a floorboard creaking) become a knock from the spirit world. Expectation can also influence our other senses as well.

Day 75

Word of the Day:

nemesis (nem´ i sis)

A. An unbeatable rival (noun)
B. A small nook or cranny
C. The Greek goddess of vengeance (noun)
D. An overwhelming number

Use #1: The Georgetown Tigers have been our football *nemesis* for many years now.
Use #2: The D.A. attacked the case almost as if she were *Nemesis*, intent upon making the guilty suffer for their crimes.

Thought of the Day:

"There are two ways to slide through life: to believe everything or to doubt everything. Both save us from thinking." *Alfred Korzybski*

Hook:

"We found him about 30 minutes ago, lying here on the floor of his locked study with a single gunshot wound to the head," said the officer to Inspector Davi. Reginald Thompson, noted mystery writer, hunter, gun enthusiast, and friend of Inspector Davi lay dead at their feet. "The note is addressed to you," he said, handing the index card to the inspector. It read:

My old friend, I have decided to end it all and you will certainly find the gun that I used. But I could not bow out without leaving you with a mystery to solve. How did I do it? To start you on your way, I would suggest you have my head x-rayed. Reginald

"Why would he suggest such a thing?" asked the officer. "It's obvious he shot himself in the head."

"Get a portable x-ray machine in here immediately," responded the inspector.

A few minutes later Davi was looking at the x-ray photo.

"Hmmmm," he mused handing the x-ray to the officer.

"But, but, but, there's no bullet!" exclaimed the officer. "He has an entry wound in his right temple, no exit wound, yet the x-ray is clear. He was found alone in a locked room. There is gunshot residue on the side of his head and his hand. He obviously shot himself but, but . . . this is the strangest thing I've ever encountered."

It had been just over an hour since they found the body. Inspector Davi began a systematic search of the house. Nothing seemed out of place, including Reginald's gun collection, except for the nine millimeter Beretta that still lay by the dead man's body. The inspector examined several firearms, carefully taking them from their cases, then replacing them as before. He worked the slide on an old Colt .45 then set it down and went into the small room where Reginald did repair work on his collection and reloaded some of his ammunition. Davi found a Smith and Wesson with a damaged breech that Reginald had obviously been working on. He ran his hand across the several bullet molds on the shelf, examined the jar of gunpowder that his friend used to reload his ammunition, and finally admired the craftsmanship of a leather holster that Reginald had made by hand.

"Any ideas, inspector?" asked the officer as Davi returned to the study.

"Yes, I know how he did it," replied the astute inspector.

What is the solution and how did Inspector Davi solve the case?

Solution:

When the inspector ran his hand over the bullet molds he noted that one had moisture on it. That mold was of the same calibre as the gun that had killed his friend. He concluded that Reginald had poured *water* into the mold and frozen it into a bullet, which he then loaded into one of the shells that he used to kill himself. The mold had by now returned to room temperature, but the cold metal had caused water from the warmer room air to condense on the mold and had not yet dried. By the time the police arrived, the bullet itself had melted, leaving nothing in poor Reginald's head but a few drops of water.

Day 76

Word of the Day:

Cassowary (cass´ o wear ee)

A. An isolated and seldom used room in a house
B. A large flightless bird of New Guinea (noun)
C. Flavorful seeds often baked onto the crust of bread
D. The deck of a passenger ship below and behind the promenade deck

Use: I saw a strange bird, a *Cassowary*, in a photo my friend in the Peace Corps sent me.

Thought of the Day:

"The society which scorns excellence in plumbing because plumbing is a humble activity—and which tolerates shoddiness in its philosophy simply because it is an exalted activity will have neither good plumbing nor good philosophy. Neither its pipes nor its ideas will hold water." *Anon*

Hook:

One morning, begin class as usual except instead of saying words aloud, simply mouth the words silently. Proceed with your lesson as usual, explaining directions, turning to the board, asking a question of a student, etc., all silently. When the class is totally confused (which will not take long), explain to them (aloud) that they have just experienced what a person who is deaf experiences every day of his or her life.

Day 77

Word of the Day:

pyrotechnics (pi ro tek´ niks)

A. Computer graphics, especially those done with vivid colors
B. Arson
C. Any structures composed of multiple layers of building materials
D. Fireworks (noun)

Derivatives: pyrotechnic, pyrotech, pyrotechnical, pyrotechnically, pyrotechny, pyrotechnist
Use: The *pyrotechnics* at the fairgrounds on the Fourth of July were absolutely breathtaking.

Thought of the Day:

"May you have the hindsight to know where you've been, the foresight to know where you're going, and the insight to know when you're going too far." *Irish Toast*

Hook:

This is a variation on the old *Cat's Cradle* string tricks we all played in grade school. However the *Freeing the Ring* trick, while simple to learn, looks impossible. Thread a looped string (you can also use a rubber band) through a ring and hold it taut between the two thumbs as in the top illustration to the left. Tell the students you will free the ring from the string while keeping the string taut and using only your two little fingers. They will, of course, say you can't do it. Complete the rest of the steps as indicated in the pictures. It takes just a little bit of practice!

Day78

Word of the Day:

precursor (pre cur´ ser)

A. A computer term meaning to backspace
B. That which precedes something else (noun)
C. In rowing, the return stroke of the oars
D. An underlayer of gravel upon which asphalt or concrete is poured

Derivative: precursory

Use: The gentle breeze that began blowing in the afternoon was simply a *precursor* to the storm that followed later that night.

Thought of the Day:

"A master can tell you what he expects of you. A teacher, however, awakens your own expectations." *Patricia Neal*

Hook:

Here's something unusual. If the students have calculators this will be even more interesting, but you can do it with just one (hopefully one that can display several digits). Start with the following problems on the board or overhead and ask them to give you the answers to each problem.

$1 \times 8 + 1 = 9$
Now, add a 2 behind the first number, multiply by 8, and add 2:
$12 \times 8 + 2 = 98$
Now, add a 3 behind the first number, multiply by 8, and add 3:
$123 \times 8 + 3 = 987$
Now, add a 4 behind the first number, multiply by 8, and add 4:
$1234 \times 8 + 4 = 9876$
See a pattern emerging? If you continue all the way to 9, you will get the series below:

$1 \times 8 + 1 = 9$
$12 \times 8 + 2 = 98$
$123 \times 8 + 3 = 987$
$1234 \times 8 + 4 = 9876$
$12345 \times 8 + 5 = 98765$
$123456 \times 8 + 6 = 987654$
$1234567 \times 8 + 7 = 9876543$
$12345678 \times 8 + 8 = 98765432$
$123456789 \times 8 + 9 = 987654321$

I don't know who worked this out, but that person must have had a lot of time on his or her hands.

Day 79

Word of the Day:

nubbin (nub´ in)

(A.) A small stunted ear of corn (noun)
B. In baseball, a slow infield ground ball
C. An old horse, especially one that has been retired from racing or work
D. A bolt of cloth or spool of thread that has been used, the remainder of which is of little or no use

Use: The family was so hungry that even a *nubbin* was a veritable feast.

Thought of the Day:

"When the mind is in a state of uncertainty, the smallest impulse may direct it to either side." *Terence*

Hook:

Here's a fun little activity to reveal the limitations of the human mind. The students may *not* use pencil and paper. They are to keep the numbers in their head.

Round 1: Say the number "96" aloud (say nine, six—not ninety-six—and say it only once), then read the following: "Edgar Allen Poe wrote the poem 'Annabel Lee'."

Now see how many can remember the number you gave them (probably all, but if any could not recall the number, they are eliminated from the next round).

Round 2: Say the number "472" then read: "Antarctica is a continent because it has land mass under the ice and snow." Again check for correct memory of the number and eliminate those who were incorrect. Follow the same procedure for each of the following rounds until all students have been eliminated.

Round 3: 8159 "Abraham Lincoln was the 16th president of the United States."

Round 4: 60738 "The capital of Albania is Tirana."

Round 5: 296415 "Did you know the 'Happy Birthday' song is copyrighted and may not be performed in public without paying a royalty fee?"

Round 6: 8240763 "In late 1958, the Kingston Trio's 'Tom Dooley' was the No. 1 song in the country."

Round 7: 20687325 "The First Amendment of the Constitution prohibits the government from establishing religion, and guarantees freedom of speech, freedom of the press, and the right to assemble and petition."

Round 8: 507412936 "A type of freewheeling jazz that was popular in the United States during the early 1900s was called Dixieland."

Round 9: 2750419638 "The mountain lion of the western United States is also called a puma."

Round 10: 73902416853 "Henry Ford did not invent the automobile, but rather was the father of the assembly line for mass producing cars at lower costs."

Anyone still in the game at this point is bordering on savant. If necessary, keep going. Below are some additional number sequences.

254198036739

9406261583746

71306075924863

It is interesting that most people drop out at about seven. Seven seems to be about the maximum number of digits we can easily remember. Ever wonder why there are no more than seven digits in your phone number (area code is a separate number—it is not added to form a 10-digit number)? Your social security number is nine digits, but notice how they break them into three digits, followed by two digits, followed by four digits instead of a continuous nine digit number.

Hmmmm, I guess I'll keep my calculator after all.

Day 80

Word of the Day:

overture (o´ va chur)

A. An attempt of a feat of great difficulty
B. An argument that takes precedence over a previous argument
C. An elevated walkway over a road
D. An opening or initial gesture or action (noun)

Derivatives: overtured, overtures, overturing
Use: The enemy made *overtures* of peace, especially after being so soundly defeated.

Thought of the Day:

"Pray to God—but keep rowing for the shore." *Old Russian Proverb*

Hook:

Here's another rebus for the students to decode.

MTOHRINNIGNG
THING
THING

Solution:

First thing in the morning (read every other letter in the top row).

Day 81

Word of the Day:

multifarious (mul ti fair´ e us)

A. Comprised of many and varied parts (adj.)
B. A story that raises suspicions
C. An ore possessing more than one mineral
D. Pertaining to being unsure of one's parentage

Derivatives: multifariously, multifariousness
Use: His *multifarious* plan was simply too complicated to possibly succeed.

Thought of the Day:

"Human history becomes more and more a race between education and catastrophe." *H.G. Wells*

Hook:

Pose this question: Is there really such a thing as motion? A motion picture contains *no* motion. It is composed of a series of rapidly projected still images. Our brain simply perceives these still images (one projected rapidly right after the other) as motion. Is it possible that motion in the real world is also really an illusion, that if we had a motion picture camera capable of taking fast enough exposures we could freeze all motion, showing that at a given infinitesimally small moment in time, any object is actually still in time and space?

Just as digital technology breaks continuous sound into a series of finite moments at which the sound is sampled and played back making it sound as if the music is continuous when, in reality, we are hearing thousands of individual *moments* or bits of sound that our brain blends together, are time and space continuous, or can they be broken down into discrete bits as well?

If so, then motion itself is nothing but an illusion and an arrow passes from one point to another by appearing completely still at a given point in time and space, then appearing completely still at the next point just beyond the first and then the next and the next, etc. And finally, what happens to the arrow between the moment at which it appears at one point in time and space and the moment at which it appears at the next? Does it actually wink out of existence for that infinitesimal moment and then wink back into existence at the next or do we simply need a camera with a faster shutter? Sort of boggles the mind, doesn't it?

Day82

Word of the Day:

coup d'etat (coo day ta´) often shortened to *coup*

A.   A French soup flavored with basil
B.   A sudden, unexpected takeover of power (noun)
C.   A wire enclosure for breeding small animals
D.   A rapid drum roll

Use: The bloodless *coup d'etat* occurred in the small island nation at 10 p.m. last night.

Thought of the Day:

"It's discouraging to consider how many people are shocked by honesty and how few by deceit." *Noel Coward*

Hook:

Water in the Hat is a trick of which almost every magician has a version. Beforehand, prepare two identical paper or plastic cups. Make sure they are of the type that has a lip around the rim. In one, carefully cut out the bottom of the cup, and on the other, carefully cut away the lip. Now the cup possessing a lip but no bottom will fit nicely into the cup with the bottom but no lip, giving the appearance of a single normal cup. (See below.)

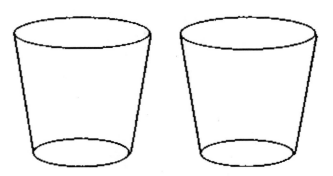

Bottom but no lip   Lip but no bottom

Borrow a hat or purse that will stand up and is deeper than the prepared cup is tall. You don't want the students to actually be able to see into the hat. The prepared cup can be sitting on the table as long as the students don't get too close of a look at it. Pick it up by the rim with your thumb on the outside and first finger on the inside of the lip. Set it in the hat or purse and tell the class you will pour water into the hat. They will look at you like this isn't much of a trick with a cup in there, so still holding the cup, scoot your thumb down a bit to separate the two cups. Now withdraw the bottomless rimmed cup and set it down being sure you don't reveal the fact that it is bottomless. Tell them it's a better trick if you don't use a cup. Proceed to pick up a pitcher of water and pour no more than half a cupful into the hat or purse. Its owner will be getting a bit uneasy by now, but tell him or her that your cup is magical and can suck up all the water you have just poured in there. Take the rimmed, bottomless cup and put it back into the hat fitting it down into the cup holding the water. Now withdraw both cups as if they were one and proceed to pour out the water to the amazement of all.

An even more amazing finish is to prepare the cups as before, using opaque cups, but insert a sponge tightly into the cup with a bottom, so it covers the bottom third of the cup and is wedged in tightly. Be careful to pour no more water into the cup than the sponge can absorb. Now when you withdraw the cup after pouring the water, have the student examine the purse or hat—no water there and with all eyes on the cup dramatically turn it upside down—no water comes out—the water has disappeared. Put the cup away or throw it in the waste can and the trick is complete. Sneaky, huh?

Day83

Word of the Day:

morose (mo ros´)

- A. Temporary
- B. Fussy
- C. Simple
- (D.) Gloomy (adj.)

Derivatives: morosely, moroseness
Use: We tried to cheer him up, but David's mood remained *morose*.

Thought of the Day:

"A ship in harbor is safe—but that is not why we build ships." *John Shedd*

Hook:

Duplicate the questionnaire on the following page and have the students fill it out. If time allows, you may wish to let them discuss and justify their rankings. There is no solution or best answer per se, but it is a good exercise in getting students to analyze the situation and evaluate their choices.

Your plane has just crashed in a South American jungle. Your three friends are injured and unable to travel. Your task is to trek to civilization and bring back help as soon as possible.

From your last known position you know only that civilization is approximately 100 miles away in a generally westward direction. In the wreckage you find the items listed below. You must first rank order them in terms of their importance in helping you to make the arduous journey ahead.

In the blank beside each item rank order its importance to your mission by placing a 1 beside most important, a 2 beside next most important, etc. When finished, if time allows, discuss and defend your rankings with your classmates.

_____ **Box of matches**

_____ **Canned food**

_____ **Silk parachute**

_____ **Backpack & frame**

_____ **.45 calibre pistol & ammo**

_____ **Anti-glare sunglasses**

_____ **Map of the area**

_____ **Six gold coins**

_____ **Flare gun**

_____ **Canteen of water**

_____ **Magnetic compass**

_____ **First aid kit**

_____ **100 feet of nylon rope**

_____ **Radio transceiver (walkie-talkie)**

_____ **Machete**

_____ **Self-inflating life raft**

Day 84

Word of the Day:

gauche (gosh) (long o)

A. A South American cowboy
B. Tactless, lacking social grace (adj.)
C. A stew, especially one made with leftovers
D. To force fit one part into another

Derivatives: gauchely, gaucheness, gaucherie
Use: Fred's *gauche* table manners led us to wonder if he had been raised in a pig sty.

Thought of the Day:

"Success is a lousy teacher. It seduces smart people into thinking they can't lose." *Bill Gates*

Hook:

How about another round of charades? Remember, only 1 minute per target.

Targets:

1. The Super Bowl

2. *Pirates of the Caribbean*

Day85

Word of the Day:

kosher (ko´ shur)

- (A.) Correct, permissible (adj.)
- B. Frightened
- C. A bird of New Zealand
- (D.) Conforming to Jewish dietary laws (adj.)

Derivatives: koshered, koshering, koshers
Use #1: Ah, ah, ah, you know that move isn't *kosher* in chess.
Use #2: Even though the dish looked delicious, Bernie had to decline because it wasn't *kosher*.

Thought of the Day:

"Great people are simply ordinary people with extraordinary determination." *Anon*

Hook:

Here are some new word/number rebuses to decode:

1. 8 S on a SS

2. 20,000 LU the S

3. 5 D in a ZC

Solutions:

1. 8 sides on a stop sign

2. *20,000 Leagues Under the Sea*

3. 5 digits in a zip code

Day86

Word of the Day:

eidolon (i dough´ lan)

A. A vagrant, bum
B. A drawing instrument used by graphic designers
C. A steep faced cliff
D. A specter or phantom (noun)

Use: The threat of war raised its ugly head like an *eidolon* determined to haunt us forever.

Thought of the Day:

"Fame is that which must be won, while honor is that which must not be lost." *Schopenhauer*

Hook:

Read to your students:

You have just been infected with a deadly virus for which there is no antidote. The virus is not communicable, but it is 100% fatal and death occurs in 24 hours. In short, you have but 24 hours to live. Question: What are the three most important things you want to do in those last 24 hours?

Give them a minute to think about it, then solicit some thoughts. Some will be funny, of course, but some will take it seriously and show real insight.

Day 87

Word of the Day:

roturier (ro tu ray´)

- A. An early photographic print on metal
- B. A scoundrel, especially a man who takes advantage of a woman's affections
- C. A deep ocean fish found in the Sea of Japan
- (D.) A person of low rank, a commoner (noun)

Use: Henry's acting as if he was of the nobility fooled no one, as his station of *roturier* was quite apparent from the beginning.

Thought of the Day:

"Take sides! Neutrality helps the oppressor, never the victim. Silence encourages the tormentor, never the tormented." *Elie Wiesel*

Hook:

Project or distribute the following logic problems:

#1: Tape 1 is longer than tape 2. Tape 6 is shorter than tape 14. Tape 12 is longer than tape 14, but shorter than tape 2. Tape 20 is longer than tape 14, but shorter than tape 12. Which tape is longest?

#2: More people use Blubbles than any other detergent. In a recent survey of women, a majority indicated they liked Blubbles best. Several movie stars, rock stars, and baseball players have endorsed Blubbles as the brand they use at home. Ergo: Blubbles is the best detergent.

Have the students discuss how these two logic problems are alike and how they are different. See if they bring up some of the points mentioned in the solution.

Solution:

#1: Tape 1 is longest. If the information given is accurate, the conclusion requires only a little analysis. The information given is all that is required to reach a logical conclusion.

#2: The conclusion reached regarding Blubbles may well be erroneous for several reasons. First: How do we know that more people use Blubbles? How was this determined? Even if true, perhaps Blubbles is simply the cheapest brand and that is why more people buy it. Maybe Blubbles spends a bundle on advertising instead of making their product better. Second: Who conducted the survey and how was it conducted? Yes, women may do laundry more often than men, but should women have been the only ones surveyed? How was majority defined? It could be that only one more than half the women surveyed liked Blubbles, and how were the women chosen who were surveyed? Maybe they only surveyed women who already liked Blubbles to begin with. How many women were surveyed? It could have been only three with two indicating they liked Blubbles best. It is also possible that a better brand of detergent is simply unavailable in the area in which the survey was conducted, so the women surveyed would know nothing about it.

Third: Let's get real! How many movie stars, rock stars, and professional athletes do their own laundry? These people are paid to endorse products. They do not do so out of the goodness of their hearts or because they genuinely believe in the quality of the product. How much faith can we put in a paid endorsement? And, who said movie stars or rock stars or professional athletes know anything about which laundry detergent is best? This is the type of invalid logic advertisers count on consumers using.

Day88

Word of the Day:

quasi (qwa´ zi)

A.   African tribe of Nigeria
B.   Sick, ill
C.   Of great value
D.   Imitation of, but not authentic (adj.)

Use: His misuse of several multi syllabic words marked him as a *quasi*-intellectual.

Thought of the Day:

"Man is the only animal that blushes—or needs to!" *Mark Twain*

Hook:

One more example of the difference between the sexes:

You will need an armless chair of standard height. A folding chair will do quite nicely. Have a boy stand feet together, heels against the wall. Place the chair about a foot in front of him, the back of the chair away from him. Now have him lean over and grab the sides of the seat of the chair. Now have him try to straighten up to his original position. Chances are he can't. Have a couple more boys try it. Men have real trouble with this. Now have a girl try it and chances are she can. Again try it with a couple of different girls. Most girls can do it.

Solution:

It's a simple matter of center of gravity. Guys have more proportionate body mass in the upper body than girls (though I'm not too sure about Dolly Parton).

Day89

Word of the Day:

piece de resistance (peez day re ze staunz´)

A. Crowning achievement (noun)
B. A small mid-afternoon snack
C. Reluctance to participate
D. A third party interceding on behalf of two lovers

Use: The chef's *piece de resistance* to a sumptuous meal was his famous cherries flambé.

Thought of the Day:

"He who asks a question is a fool for five minutes. He who does not ask a question remains a fool forever." *Chinese Proverb*

Hook:

This is kind of interesting: Everybody is aware of whether they are right- or left-handed. How many are aware of whether they are right- or left-eyed? To determine eye preference, with both eyes open and your arm extended, point your right finger at something in the room at least 15 or 20 feet away. Now close your left eye. Does your finger still point directly at the object? Try closing your right eye (leaving the left one open—otherwise it may be hard to see anything). Again, is your finger still pointing directly at the object or does it appear to be pointing slightly off to the side? Whichever eye is open when you appear to be pointing directly at the object is your eye preference.

Day90

Word of the Day:

beatific (be a tif´ ik)

A. In rhythm
B. Joyous (adj.)
C. Unusual
D. Humble

Derivative: beatifically
Use: Her *beatific* smile lit up the whole room.

Thought of the Day:

"I have not failed. Instead, I have succeeded at finding ten thousand ways that won't work." *Thomas Alva Edison*

Hook:

Here's one the students just won't believe the first time they see it. Take an empty glass soda bottle and fill the mouth with modeling clay. Then stick a toothpick into the clay vertically so approximately 2 inches or so sticks out. (Flat toothpicks can be made to work but the round toothpicks are stronger and easier to use.) Get two metal table forks (plastic will break and is too light). Stick the tines together firmly and then stick a second toothpick into the tines as shown. Make sure the toothpick is firmly wedged.

Now you are ready for some magic. Carefully place the tip of the toothpick sticking out of the forks onto the tip of the toothpick sticking out of the modeling clay and voilá, they balance (you may have to experiment with the angle the toothpick protrudes from the fork tines, but if you practice this a time or two you can do it easily). Looking at the photo below, you see the same thing your students will see—a seemingly impossible balancing act:

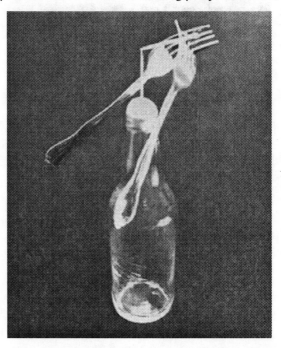

Of course there is no trick at all. Any fulcrum has to have equal mass on either side in order to balance. The fulcrum here is the vertical toothpick. If you examine it carefully, from any angle, you will find the amount of mass (forks) is equal on either side of the fulcrum. It does look funny though, doesn't it?

Day91

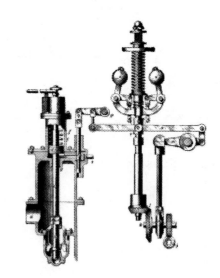

Word of the Day:

harangue (ha rang´)

A. A light, fluffy dessert made with beaten eggs
B. A military utility belt
C. An outcropping of rock near the top of a cliff
D. A long-winded tirade (noun)

Derivatives: harangued, haranguing, haranguer
Use: His overbearing *harangue* in front of the assembly seemed endless.

Thought of the Day:

"In the long course of history, having people understand each other is much greater security than another tank, bomber, or nuclear submarine." *William Fulbright*

Hook:

Try another round of *Once Upon a Time* (see Day 52). Give the student the four words below. Give him or her a few moments to compose a story using the four words. The student then has only 1 minute to tell the story containing all four words. Then see if the class can tell which words were the four target words.

Target words: computer chip, antique, walking stick, clown

Day 92

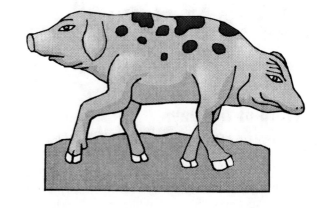

Word of the Day:

somnolent (som´ na lent)

A. Pensive, thoughtful
B. Drowsy, sleepy (adj.)
C. Fretful, restless
D. Nonexistent

Derivatives: somnolence, somnolently
Use: The long winded speeches, teamed with the fact I did not get much sleep last night, led to a *somnolent* afternoon.

Thought of the Day:

"Young people are not as vessels to be filled, but rather as candles to be lit."
Robert Shaffer

Hook:

Here's one that looks as if it's nothing but math, but the kids don't have to calculate anything, they just have to find some faulty reasoning. Announce you have just made an important discovery. You have discovered that one is equal to two. The students will scoff, of course. Then tell them you'll prove it. Go through this step by step on the board explaining the process as you go:

1. Let $X = 1$
2. Then, of course, $X=X$
3. Square both sides: $X^2 = X^2$
4. Subtract X^2 from both sides: $X^2 - X^2 = X^2 - X^2$
5. Factor both sides: $X(X-X) = (X+X)(X-X)$
6. Factor out the $(X-X)$: $X = (X+X)$
7. $X = 2X$
8. Ergo: $1=2$

See if they can catch the faulty operation.

Solution:

The flaw is in line six. You are dividing both sides of the equation by zero, a forbidden mathematical operation. Any number divided by zero is zero. So the equation should end up: $0 = 0$. It's easy to miss this one.

Day 93

Word of the Day:

au naturel (o not shur all´)

A. Any neutral color
B. In a natural state, unadulterated (adj./adv.)
C. Gifted with a special talent
D. Nude (adj./adv.)

Use #1: The stately trees had stood *au naturel* for centuries. (adv.)
Use #2: Needless to say, the *au naturel* model garnered a lot of attention. (adj.)

Thought of the Day:

"Knowledge is not a commodity. It is never used up; rather it increases by diffusion and grows by dispersion." *Daniel Boorstin*

Hook:

Here's a rather zany paradox (and a great book).

This paradox comes from the novel *Catch 22* by Joseph Heller. The story takes place in WWII at an American air base where bomber losses are staggering. Orr, a character in the story, wants to be grounded so he won't have to fly because he insists, "Those Germans are trying to kill me!" The base doctor tells Orr that if he is crazy, the doctor can ground him—all Orr has to do is ask to be grounded. But the minute he asks to be grounded, it means he is sane, because only a crazy man would want to fly more missions. Ergo: Orr must keep flying, because if he flies the missions, he is crazy and doesn't have to, but if he doesn't want to, he is sane and therefore has to. (It's a dark, zany, and wonderful book, by the way.)

Solution:

Unfortunately for Orr, there is no solution. The poor guy had to keep flying (although, ultimately he did find a solution to his dilemma if not the paradox—no, you'll just have to read the book).

Day94

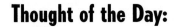

Word of the Day:

shoal(s) (shol) (long o)

A. A 3-year-old filly
B. A schedule or timetable
C. Shallow water (noun)
D. A hand tool for shaping wood

Derivatives: shoaled, shoaling
Use: We waded out into the *shoals* to find some shells that might have come in with the tide.

Thought of the Day:

"Affection can withstand very severe storms of vigor, but never a long polar frost of indifference." *Sir Walter Scott*

Hook:

Engineers can sometimes be too smart for their own good. The following joke was sent to me by an engineer friend of mine.

Three Americans, a cab driver, a window washer, and an engineer, are captured in a strange land and, after a kangaroo court trial, are sentenced to die by the guillotine (no, I don't know why and the ACLU was nowhere in sight). The cab driver is led up the steps. His last request is to be executed looking to heaven, so he is placed facing upward in the rack and the order given to drop the blade. Yet, when the lever was pulled, the blade simply did not drop. The high priest overseeing the execution declared it a divine miracle and the cab driver was pardoned and released. The window washer also requested to be placed in the rack face-up. Again the command was given, the lever was pulled and yet again the blade refused to drop. Again the priest declared it divine intervention and the window washer was released as well. Now it was the engineer's turn. Following suit he also asked to be placed in the rack looking skyward. Just as the order was ready to be given to pull the lever, the engineer shouted, "Wait! Wait! I see the trouble! The rope is too large. It's slipping out of the groove and binding the pulley!"

Day 95

Word of the Day:

garret (gaer´ it)

(A.) An attic or loft (noun)
B. To strangle
C. To run through with a sword
D. A cane or walking stick

Use: We made our way up to the *garret* where the old trunk sat forlornly in the dust.

Thought of the Day:

"I have a dream that someday we will live in a nation where people will not be judged by the color of their skin, but by the content of their character."
Martin Luther King, Jr.

Hook:

Here's another logic puzzle for students to figure out:

Four people who live on Whimple Street decided to do some spring repairs. From the information below, determine who lives in each house and did which repair to the property.

1. The person who fixed the front railing is Margie's next door neighbor.

2. Perry lives two doors east of the person who sowed grass seed.

3. The person who made shutter repairs lives next door to, and west, of Kirk.

4. Bonnie, who doesn't live in a corner house, isn't the one who made repairs to the garage.

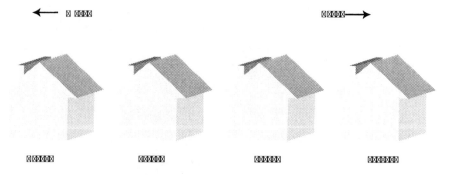

Solution:

Brick: Margie, seed; Frame: Bonnie, railing; Stone: Perry, shutters; Stucco: Kirk, garage

Day 96

Word of the Day:

felicity (fe lis´ i tee)

A. Faithfulness
B. Genuineness
C. Fortuitousness, serendipity
D. Great happiness, bliss (noun)

Derivatives: felicific, felicitate, felicitator, felicitation, felicitously, felicitousness
Use: The fates had seemed to smile upon Nancy and her heart was filled with *felicity*.

Thought of the Day:

"Science has proof without certainty. Religion has certainty without proof."
Montague

Hook:

Here's an interesting optical illusion: Project the figure below, and then ask the students which is longer, line AX or line AY?

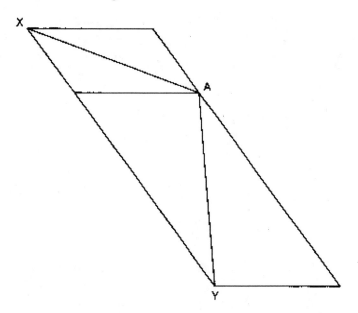

For a full-sized reproducible of this image, see Appendix, page 215.

Solution:

Although line AY appears longer, they are both the same length. The line bisecting angle XAY produces a much smaller area on the top of the figure as opposed to the bottom. This fools the eye and brain into thinking that the line bisecting that smaller area must be shorter than the line bisecting the larger area.

Day 97

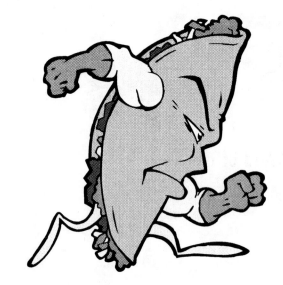

Word of the Day:

Lilliputian (lil i pew´ shun)

A. Exaggerated, over emphasized
B. A person who is strict, unyielding
C. Very small (noun/adj.)
D. Pertaining to a smooth flowing liquid

Derivative: The word is derived from the tiny island inhabitants in Johnathan Swift's *Gulliver's Travels*.
Use #1: Her stature was so short, she could have been a *Lilliputian*. (noun)
Use #2: Her *Lilliputian* stature made her stand out among the other students. (adj.)

Thought of the Day:

"Sow an act and you reap a habit; sow a habit and you reap character; sow character and you reap your destiny." *Frances Willard*

Hook:

You have 10 glasses set before you in a row. The first five glasses are full of water. The other five are empty. Can you move just two glasses to create a row in which the empty and full glasses alternate?

Solution:

Try this out of the box thinking: Pick up glass number 2 and empty it into glass number 7. Then pick up glass 4 and empty it into glass number 9.

Day 98

Word of the Day:

avant-garde (ah vaunt gard´)

A. A king or queen's royal military escort
B. Ultramodern, establishing a trend (noun/adj.)
C. Unruly, undisciplined
D. Sudden, without warning

Use #1: The movement was so ground breaking, it was definitely considered *avant-garde*. (noun)
Use #2: The *avant-garde* painting left everyone with their mouth agape. (adj.)

Thought of the Day:

"One must reach beyond awareness of things, which is merely knowledge, to awareness of others, which is wisdom, and thence to awareness of self, which is enlightenment." *Richard Fraher*

Hook:

Once upon a time someone combined the idea of roller skates with a surfboard and the skateboard was born. Now it's your turn: Brainstorm to see how many new products you can create by combining existing products or ideas.

Day 99

Word of the Day:

heteronym (het´ er a nim)

(A.) Words spelled the same but pronounced differently and with different meanings (noun)
B. Words spelled differently but pronounced the same
C. Words spelled and pronounced the same but with different meanings
D. Words spelled differently but with similar meanings

Use: This *heteronym* will serve as an example: The archer lowered his bow, then executed a deep bow to the queen.

Thought of the Day:

"You can put dope or hope in your brains. You should know, however, that it is not your aptitude, but your attitude which will affect your altitude." *Jesse Jackson*

Hook:

Here are some more paraphrases to decode:

1. Ascending from one level of existence to another through studied cognitive reflection.

2. Ananas comosus inverted baked agglutinous pastry.

3. A vision while at physiological rest occurring during the nocturnal median period between the solstice and the equinox.

Solution:

1. Transcendental Meditation

2. Pineapple upside down cake

3. *A Midsummer Night's Dream*

Day 100

Word of the Day:

juxtapose (jux ta poz´) (long o)

A. To play a trick or practical joke
B. To switch positions
C. To authenticate
D. To place side by side (verb)

Derivatives: juxtaposed, juxtaposing, juxtaposes
Use: It was much easier to compare the two photographs once they had been *juxtaposed*.

Thought of the Day:

"Nothing great was ever accomplished without enthusiasm." *Ralph Waldo Emerson*

Hook:

Tell your students you are going to teach them the three most wonderful words in the world and that you will do it without writing or speaking. Use the sign below. You might even get them interested in learning to sign.

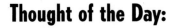

The sign above is that for "I love you." With the thumb, index, and little finger extended, move the hand toward the person.

Day 101

Word of the Day:

munificent (mew nif´ i cent)

A. Talkative
B. Error prone
C. Generous (adj.)
D. Urban as opposed to rural in nature

Derivatives: munificence, munificently

Use: It was only as a result of the *munificent* donation of the corporation that the city was able to complete the park.

Thought of the Day:

"Like a ten-speed bike, most of us have gears we have never used" *Charles Schulz*

Hook:

Project or duplicate the following material:

You are an agent working for Homeland Security. You have received a tip that a terrorist is aboard Flight 788 that just landed. The following people, about whom you have been given some scanty information, get off the plane. Put a 1 beside the person you would search first, a 2 beside the person you would search second, etc., until you have numbered all the possible suspects.

_____ Mrs. Edwina Stanton: White American, age 32, housewife.

_____ Dr. Raul Sanchez: Mexican American, age 64, medical doctor

_____ Gina LeMay: Black Muslim American, age 28, nurse

_____ Hikim Ali Budeen: Saudi, age 22, exchange student

_____ Pierre DePew: French, age 36, importer/exporter

_____ Jeanie Spencer: White American, age 15, high school student

_____ Edmund Wellington: English, age 42, college professor

_____ May Ling Chow: Chinese, age 20, exchange student

_____ Naomi Mobutto, Nigerian, age 27, fashion designer

_____ Alexi Durapov, Russian, age 45, newspaper reporter

When the students are finished, have them set the first list aside. Now they are to rank the same people placing a 1 beside the person least like them, a 2 beside the person next least like them, etc. until the list is complete. Then have them compare lists. What they have done in the first list is called profiling, creating a mental image of who might commit a terrorist act (or anything else). In the second, of course, they have simply exposed their own biases. Now have them compare the two lists. Chances are the two lists are going to look very much the same. The truth is, from the scanty information given, there is no way we could logically have any more reason to suspect one person than another on the list, yet we all allowed our irrational biases, not reason, to dictate (and in our minds justify) singling out certain individuals to subject to search and seizure. If there is enough time, this might provide a springboard for a discussion of prejudice and how it can feed upon fear.

For a reproducible of this activity, see Appendix, page 216.

Day 102

Word of the Day:

prodigal (prod´ i gul)

A. Absent for an extended period
B. Wasteful, extravagant (adj.)
C. Last born
D. Hateful, despicable

Derivative: prodigally
Use: Ben's *prodigal* lifestyle will eventually land him in the poorhouse.

Thought of the Day:

"The fragrance remains in the hand that gives the rose." *Heda Bejar*

Hook:

Here's one to get them thinking:

Mary and Ron visited her uncle's farm. Mary liked the chickens, while Ron's favorite were the horses. When they were on their way home they began wondering how many chickens and how many horses they had seen.

"Did you count them?" asked Ron.

"Not exactly, but I can tell you this: The total number of horses and chickens we saw had 30 eyes and 44 feet."

Determine how many chickens and how many horses they saw.

Solution:

30 eyes means 15 total animals. If all 15 animals stand on two feet, there would be 30 feet on the ground, but there are a total of 44 feet, which means 14 horse feet are in the air. Ergo: 7 horses and 8 chickens.

Day 103

Word of the Day:

supererogate (sue per air´ o gate)

A. To create an oxygen-rich atmosphere
B. Sentencing to more than one life term
C. To speak eloquently
D. To do more than is required or expected (verb)

Derivatives: supererogated, supererogating, supererogates, supererogation, supererogatory, supererogative
Use: Tracy is such a hard worker. She almost always *supererogates*, regardless of how hard or how long the job will take.

Thought of the Day:

"Never worry about failing—worry about the chances you'll miss if you don't even try." *Anon*

Hook:

A new drug has just been introduced on the market that will prevent all forms of cancer. It has a side effect, however. It lowers your IQ. How many points of IQ would you be willing to give up to be guaranteed that you would be cancer free for the rest of your life? You may get some surprising responses.

Day 104

Word of the Day:

exsanguinate (ek sang´ gwa nate)

(A.) To drain blood (verb)
B. To flavor with spicy seasoning
C. To pine over a lost love
D. To withdraw from competition in anticipation of being disqualified

Derivatives: exsanguinated, exsanguinating, exsanguinates, exsanguine, exsanguinous
Use: One of the first steps in embalming is to *exsanguinate* the body.

Thought of the Day:

"If the only tool you have is a hammer, you tend to treat everything as if it were a nail." *Baruch*

Hook:

Try this puzzler:

Thaddeus was 20 years old in 1999 but only 15 years old in 2004. How can this be?

Solution:

Thaddeus was born in 2019 B.C., making him 20 years old in 1999 B.C. and 15 years old in 2004 B.C. Tsk, tsk, tsk, assumed it was A.D. did we?

Day 105

Word of the Day:

remonstrate (re mon´ strate) (long a)

A. Demonstrate again for clarification
B. To protest or oppose (verb)
C. To accept blame or responsibility
D. To scream or yell

Derivatives: remonstrated, remonstrating, remonstrates, remonstration, remonstrative, remonstrator

Use: The protesters began to *remonstrate* the removal of the stately trees as the bulldozers began their destructive work.

Thought of the Day:
Hook:

"When all else fails—try following directions." *Anon*

This is a neat illusion. It works better if you can duplicate the page in color and distribute it to each student, but it will also work, to a lesser degree, by projecting it onto a white screen in a darkened room, then simultaneously turning off the projector and turning on the room lights, or you can scan the images onto a computer screen, have the students look intently for 30 seconds then look onto a white sheet of paper. The next paragraph describes using paper copies.

With the room lights on, distribute the page to each student along with a blank white sheet of paper. Have the students place the white sheet next to the sheet with the dots. Now have the students stare at the dots for 30 seconds. Tell them to look only at the dots and try to keep their eyes from wandering. You can keep time for them. When you give the signal they are to look directly at the blank white paper. No, they won't see Elvis, but they will see some afterimages in some strange colors.

You and your students may wish to experiment with various color combinations. Why do some combinations work and others don't? Why does the effect diminish if you keep repeating it? You might want to borrow a color wheel from the art teacher or have the students take their questions to the art teacher. This should make you very popular with the art teacher.

Solution:

Notice the afterimages? These are caused by fatiguing of the receptors in our eyes.

For a full-size reproducible of this image, see Appendix, page 217.

Day 106

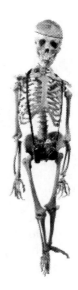

Word of the Day:

talisman (tal´ is mun)

- A. A town crier
- B. A spinner of tales, story teller
- C. An object thought to possess magical powers (noun)
- D. The dealer in a card game

Derivative: talismanic
Use: He futilely rubbed the *talisman*, hoping to ward off the eerie specter that confronted him.

Thought of the Day:

"There have been just as many martyrs for bad causes as for good ones."
H. W. Van Loon

Hook:

Your meal calls for 15 minutes of cooking, but the only timers you have are a 7 minute sand glass and an 11 minute sand glass. How can you time 15 minutes correctly using these two timepieces?

Solution:

Start both sand glasses when you begin cooking the meal. When the 7 minute glass is empty, turn it over and start it again. When the 11 minute glass is empty, turn the 7 minute glass over. It will now have four more minutes to run. When the 7 minute glass empties, your 15 minutes are up.

Day 107

Word of the Day:

jambeau (jam´ bo) (long o)

A. A Creole festive celebration with food and music
B. A decorative type of embroidery stitch
C. A French cooking utensil
D. Lower leg armor of the medieval period (noun)

Use: From helmet to *jambeau*, the knight stood in stately splendor.

Thought of the Day:

"To fear love is to fear life, and those who fear life are already three parts dead." *Bertrand Russell*

Hook:

This little exercise will get them analyzing and evaluating without even realizing it. Announce to the class:

A new regulation is being considered that will require all cars to be made from an identical design (body, engine, interior, features, etc.). Brainstorm in small groups for 2 minutes, listing as many advantages and disadvantages to this idea as you possibly can. Your list must contain both.

If time allows ask them if, overall, this would be a good idea. Why? Why not?

Day 108

Word of the Day:

quisling (quiz´ ling)

A. Baby duck
B. A question that has no answer
C. A traitor (noun)
D. A flagpole

Use: That *quisling* has sold us out to the enemy!

Thought of the Day:

"When baiting a mousetrap with cheese, always leave room for the mouse."
Anon

Hook:

Inspector Davi noted the sign over the door of the small shop: **R. D. Cummins: Antiques and Gold Coins**. Entering, he heard a rustle in the back of the store, then a young man in his mid-twenties came through the curtain that separated the store from the living quarters in back.

"I'd like to see Ms. Cummins, the proprietor, please," stated the inspector.

"My aunt is ill. She's resting at the moment," was the reply.

"Martina and I are old friends," said the inspector. "I hope it's nothing too serious."

"No, just a touch of the flu. I've been helping out for the last few days, until she gets to feeling better."

"Well, even knowing what a recluse she tends to be, being an only child and never marrying and all, I'm sure she appreciates your help."

"I'm just glad to do what I can. Could I help you with anything?"

"Well, I just need some advice. A friend of mine asked me about authenticating some Roman coins. I couldn't answer his questions, but I was sure Martina could. Perhaps you could just ask her a quick question for me."

"Glad to."

"Does the B.C. go before or after the number? In other words, should the date on the coin read 35 B.C. or B.C. 35?"

"I'll go ask her and be right back," said the young man. "I'd let you ask her yourself, but she said she doesn't want to give this bug to anyone else." Momentarily the young man returned smiling. "She said the number always comes first. It should read 35 B.C."

"You're under arrest," said the inspector, slapping handcuffs on the startled young man. Ms. Cummins was found tied and gagged in the back room. The young man had obviously intended to rob her and had been interrupted by the inspector. What three things made the inspector suspicious?

Solution:

1. Even though Ms. Cummins' initials on the door read R. D. Cummins, the inspector referred to her as Martina, which obviously was not her name. Yet the young man said nothing.

2. The inspector knew that Ms. Cummins was an only child and never married. Ergo: she could not be anyone's aunt.

3. No coin could bear a B.C. (before Christ) date because no one could have known ahead of time when Christ would be born. Ms. Cummins, a true coin expert, would have known this and said so if the young man had really asked her.

Day 109

Word of the Day:

retinue (ret´ in you)

A. An accounting term referring to profit margin
B. Those who accompany a person of wealth or fame (noun)
C. Afterimages in the eye
D. A posse or group of vigilantes

Use: The rock star arrived to the usual fanfare with her ever present *retinue*.

Thought of the Day:

"Wisdom is considered a sign of weakness by the powerful because a wise man can lead without power, but only a powerful man can lead without wisdom." *Mark Cohen*

Hook:

What do the following words have in common?

DEFENDING
CALMNESS
SIGHING
CANOPY
STUMBLE

Solution:

Each has three letters in alphabetical order.

Day 110

Word of the Day:

edify (ed´ i fi)

A.   To eat or devour completely
B.   To inform or enlighten (verb)
C.   To attach one's signature to a document
D.   To prove beyond doubt

Derivatives: edifying, edified, edifies, edifier
Use: Now if I may have your attention, I will attempt to *edify* each and every one of you.

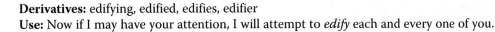

Thought of the Day:

"Democracy substitutes election by the incompetent many for appointment by the corrupt few." *G. B. Shaw*

Hook:

You are given two closed metal cylinders that are identical in appearance and weight. The only difference is that one is solid, made of a lighter alloy, while the other is hollow, constructed of a heavier metal. You may not drill into or alter the cylinders in any way. How can you determine which is hollow and which is solid?

Solution:

There are several ways it can be done. The easiest is to roll the cylinders across the floor. The hollow cylinder will roll farther. In physics they call it a higher moment of inertia because its mass is located around the rim as opposed to the center (like you wanted to know that).

Day 111

Word of the Day:

draconian (dray co´ ne an)

- (A.) Severe, harsh (adj.)
- B. Pertaining to dragons
- C. Referring to the 15th century
- D. Extraordinary, rare

Derivatives: draconically, draconic
Use: The officer's *draconian* style of leadership was soon telling on his crew.

Thought of the Day:

"Being right half the time beats being half right all the time." *Anon*

Hook:

A work train, made up of a locomotive and five cars, stops at a small station. The station has a small siding that can hold only the engine and two cars. A passenger train is due traveling in the same direction. How do they let it through?

Solution:

The work train backs into the siding and uncouples three cars. The locomotive and the other two cars then pull up further on the track. The passenger train pulls past the siding, then stops, backs up, and couples to the three cars on the siding. The passenger train now pulls onto the main line, then backs up, allowing the work train locomotive and its two cars to back into the siding. The passenger train now uncouples the three work train cars and proceeds on its way leaving the work train locomotive to pull onto the track, back up, recouple the three cars and be on its way as well.

Day 112

Word of the Day:

hermetic (her met´ ik)

A. Pertaining to heat
B. Brave, heroic
C. Completely sealed, impervious (adj.)
D. Pertaining to the time period of the Trojan War

Derivatives: hermetical, hermetically

Use: The seal had been *hermetic*, so even though the sample had been under water for almost a hundred years, it was perfectly preserved.

Thought of the Day:

"Only the weak blame parents, race, the times, society, or fate. Everyone has it within his or her power to say: *This* I am today; *that* I will be tomorrow." *Louis L'amour*

Hook:

Set up three beakers of water; one at room temperature, one as hot as can be stood without burning the skin, and one filled with ice water. Have two students come forward, one placing his finger or hand (depending on the size of the beakers) in the hot water, while the other student places hers in the ice water. Have them keep their hands in their respective beakers for at least 30 seconds. Then have them suddenly immerse that hand in the room temperature water and ask each what the new water feels like. Chances are one will say "cold" or "cool" while the other will say "hot" or "warm."

Solution:

It brings up the interesting question: Does *hot* and *cold* mean the same to everyone? At what temperature would an Eskimo say "it's cold outside"? At what temperature would a Fiji Islander say "it's hot outside"? Would those coincide with our own sense of cold and hot?

Day 113

Word of the Day:

recourse (re´ korss)

A. A revision or modification
B. An argument
C. An opportunity for action (noun)
D. A change of direction

Use: With no other options open, our only *recourse* was to adopt the plan as submitted.

Thought of the Day:

"The universe is full of magical things, patiently waiting for our wits to grow sharper." *Eden Phillpotts*

Hook:

Two winemakers examined a barrel of wine.

"This barrel is more than half full," said one.

"Oh no," said the other, "it's less than half full."

Without using measuring devices of any kind, how could they tell?

Solution:

Remove the top and tip the barrel until the wine is level with the top (as shown).

If you can see any part of the bottom of the barrel (as shown), the barrel is less than half full. If you cannot see the bottom at all, the barrel is more than half full.

Day 114

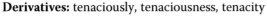

Word of the Day:

tenacious (ten a´ shus)

(A.) Persistent
B. Infected with a disease
C. Without a place to live, homeless
D. In music, to be played loudly

Derivatives: tenaciously, tenaciousness, tenacity
Use: It was only his *tenacious* nature that enabled Gary to finally make the team as a walk-on.

Thought of the Day:

"Man is the most formidable of all the beasts of prey and indeed the only one which preys systematically on its own species." *William James*

Hook:

Here's a rebus to solve.

BENCHED 52 CARDS

Solution:

Not playing with a full deck.

Day 115

Word of the Day:

sordid (sor´ did)

A. A slightly irregular circle
B. Composed of a variety of parts
C. A three handed poker game
D. Depraved, unsavory (adj.)

Derivatives: sordidly, sordidness
Use: The *sordid* nature of the movie led to its being banned in most movie theaters.

Thought of the Day:

"Conscience, the same as judgment, may be erroneous." *Hobbes*

Hook:

The *French Drop* or *French Pass* is probably the first trick that every magician learns and can be done with a minimum of practice. Take a small coin or other small object (the smaller the better to start with) and hold it between the thumb and first finger of the right hand showing it to the audience with the palm turned toward you. Now bring the left hand down to cover the coin, thumb, and finger, as if you are grabbing the coin. As the left hand covers the right, the coin is released (unseen by the audience) and drops into the palm of the right hand where the last three fingers close around it. The left hand now closes as if containing the coin. The index finger of the right hand is left straight and as the two hands separate, the closed left hand is turned upward with the index finger of the right hand pointing toward it. This directs attention to the empty left hand. Now tap the left hand with the right index finger (or you can have a student blow on the left hand) open the hand with a flourish and reveal the coin has disappeared.

There are many variations of how to make the coin reappear. The simplest is to quickly reach behind the ear of a student with your right hand and move the coin between your thumb and index finger once again. Withdraw the hand holding the coin, wondering aloud how in the world it got behind the student's ear.

Another return is to have a small glass jar at your side. Tell the students the coin has simply turned invisible but by throwing it into the air it will regain its original form. With the empty left hand, pretend to throw the coin into the air. At the moment when the students look up, grab the jar with your left hand near the top of the jar and bring your right hand also to the top near the rim wedging the coin between the palm and jar, very close to the rim. Now look upward, yell "Here it comes!", raise the jar as if to catch the coin, and let the jar suddenly drop as if the weight of the coin has caused this to

135

happen and as this is done, let the coin quickly tip over into the jar. It will arrive with a clink. Nice trick, but it will require some practice.

The French Pass can be performed for extremely young children (who are fooled a little more easily) with only a few minutes practice. If you expect to fool high school students, a bit more practice is necessary. ***Warning***: Don't do the trick more than once unless you want them to catch on as to how the trick is done.

Day 116

Word of the Day:

quagmire (kwag´ mir) (long i)

A. A rug from any of a number of Middle Eastern countries
B. A European folk dance performed barefoot to lively music
C. A difficult, virtually impossible situation (noun)
D. A military dress uniform

Use: Vietnam quickly became a political and military *quagmire* for the United States.

Thought of the Day:

"If our foresight were as good as our hindsight, we'd all be better off a damn (darn) sight." *Anon*

Hook:

Here's a stumper.

Late one night a woman came home, entered her living room, and switched on the the light. She was distressed to find the remains of her husband lying near the fireplace. He had committed suicide. Yet, she ignored the situation entirely, made herself a cup of tea before beginning some housework, with nary a call to the police or the coroner. What could explain her strange behavior?

Solution:

Her husband had killed himself 3 years earlier. The urn, containing his cremated ashes, had been knocked from the fireplace mantle by her cat and had scattered on the floor.

Day 117

Word of the Day:

bibliotics (bib lee ot´ iks)

A. Those who study the Bible and its teachings
B. Computer errors caused by degradation of components in the hard drive
C. The collective processes in wine fermentation
D. The examination of documents to verify authenticity and authorship (noun)

Use: Through the use of *bibliotics* we were able to determine the document, which was claimed to be the diary of Adolf Hitler, was actually a fraud.

Thought of the Day:

"In many ways the saying *know thyself* is lacking. It is far better to know other people." *Menander*

Hook:

Ms. Wilson was expecting a delivery of flowers, but, having to be gone, she stuck a note to her door. The note read:

The doorbell to my apartment is not working so please use the knocker. If I am not at home, try ringing the doorbell of my next door neighbor and you may leave them with him. If he isn't home, you can leave them with my aunt who lives in apartment 6B.

Unfortunately, after Ms. Wilson left, the note fell off her door, so when the floral delivery person arrived he found the note lying in the hall, unsure from which door it had fallen (see diagram). Yet, with a little reasoning he was able to deliver the flowers successfully. Which door is Ms. Wilson's and how did he figure it out?

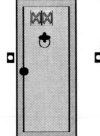  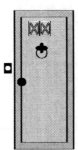 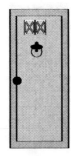 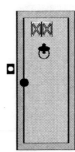 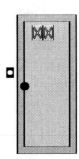

Solution:

The apartments with both doorbells *and* knockers are 6A, 6C, and 6E. We know Ms. Wilson's door has both a knocker and a doorbell, but 6A and 6C cannot be hers because their only neighbor with a doorbell is 6B and we know from the note that Ms. Wilson's aunt lives there. Ergo: Ms. Wilson must live in 6E.

Day 118

Word of the Day:

kerf (kurf)

   A.   A two masted sailing ship
   B.   The groove made by an axe or saw (noun)
   C.   The second, minute, or hour hands of a clock
   D.   A direction indicating away from the wind

Use: No matter how hard I chopped, with the axe as dull as it was, the *kerf* seemed to get no deeper.

Thought of the Day:

"The rung of the ladder is not meant as a rest, but rather a means to hold one foot to enable you to put the other somewhat higher." *T. H. Huxley*

Hook:

Divide the figure below into four figures, identical in shape and area.

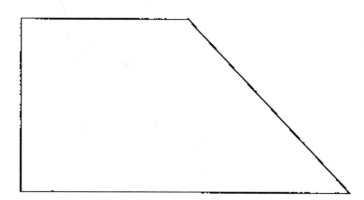

Solution:

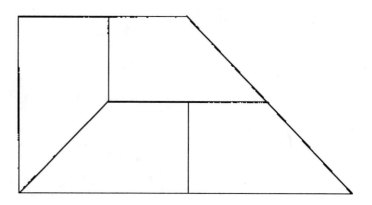

Day 119

Word of the Day:

beguile (be gil´) (long i)

A. The capital of Belgium
B. To captivate, cast a spell over (verb)
C. To confuse, befuddle
D. The largest of the Canary Islands

Derivatives: beguiling, beguiled, beguiles, beguilement, beguiler
Use: With those dreamy eyes and soft seductive voice, she can *beguile* almost any boy she meets.

Thought of the Day:

"Being defeated is often a temporary condition. Giving up is what makes it permanent." *Marilyn Vos Savant*

Hook:

Mr. Bumpkis has three steaks to grill. His grill, however, will hold only two steaks at a time. Each side of the steak must be cooked for 10 minutes, making a total of 20 minutes per steak. What is the least amount of time necessary for Mr. Bumpkis to grill the three steaks and how is it done?

Solution:

Let's call the three steaks A, B, and C, each having a side 1 and a side 2. For the first 10 minutes cook A1 and B1. For the second 10 minutes put steak B aside and cook sides A2 and C1. Steak A is now finished, so it is removed. Cook B2 and C2 and the steaks are finished in 30, not 40 minutes.

Day120

Word of the Day:

smirch (smurch) or *besmirch* (be smurch´)

A. Smile
B. Act in a pompous or superior manner
C. Press under a flat weight
D. To smear or dishonor someone's reputation (verb)

Derivatives: besmirched, besmircher, besmirching, besmirches, besmirchment
Use: Bill's vehement verbal attack made it obvious to everyone that he was trying to *smirch* (*besmirch*) Allie.

Thought of the Day:

"A lesson which all history teaches those who are wise: put your trust in ideas—not circumstances." *Emerson*

Hook:

A bit of history and a puzzle: On November 24, 1971, a man calling himself D. B. Cooper hijacked a Northwest airliner in flight from Portland to Seattle declaring he had a bomb. When the plane landed for refueling, he demanded $200,000 and four parachutes. These were delivered, he released the passengers, but kept the crew aboard and the plane took off headed to Mexico as he instructed. While in flight he strapped on one of the parachutes, lowered a rear ramp and jumped with the money into the night. He was never seen again and his disappearance is one of the great mysteries of the 20th century. The question is, why did he demand four parachutes when his intention was only to use one? The other three parachutes were left aboard the plane untouched.

Solution:

By demanding four parachutes, he gave the impression that he would be forcing some of the other passengers or crew to also jump. With that as a possibility, the authorities did not dare tamper with any of the chutes and so Cooper was assured of getting a working chute with which to make his escape.

Day 121

Word of the Day:

lament (la mint´)

A. An official decree
B. To express mourning, grief, or regret (verb)
C. To layer two or more plys together
D. The process whereby mammals produce milk for their young

Derivatives: lamented, lamenting, laments, lamenter, lamentation, lamentable, lamentably, lamentedly
Use: We all *lamented* the death of the legendary jazz pianist.

Thought of the Day:

"To sin by silence when we should protest—makes cowards of us all."
Abraham Lincoln

Hook:

This is a neat trick:

For *Calendar Magic*, you will need a standard calendar. It doesn't even have to be a current one. Have a student choose any month from the calendar without telling you what month has been chosen. Have the student draw a square box around any four dates as in the illustration (two adjacent dates and the two dates directly under them).

Now have the student add the four selected numbers together. In our example above, the answer is 48. Have him or her announce the total to the class. Now you announce that knowing only the sum of those four numbers you know which dates were selected. When you correctly tell the dates, the students will be amazed. Here's how to do it:

Whatever the sum the student announces, divide by 4 and then subtract 4—this gives you the lowest number. For instance, in our example we take the sum of 48, divide by 4 and arrive at 12, then subtract 4 and we have 8, the lowest of the four numbers. We now add 1 to get 9, the next number, and add 7 to each of those first two numbers, which gives us 15 and 16 respectively. It always works. Give it a try.

Day 122

Word of the Day:

crux (krux)

A. Cross shaped
B. The essential or critical part (noun)
C. A plan to divert attention
D. A vessel for smelting steel

Derivative: cruxes
Use: Let's agree to stop beating around the bush and get to the *crux* of the problem.

Thought of the Day:

"Measure wealth not by the things you have—but by the things you have for which you would not take money." *Anon*

Hook:

Most would agree that at the South Pole you cannot look south and at the North Pole you cannot look north. But where would you be if you could look north or south but could not look either east or west?

Solution:

The center of the earth. There you could still look up or down (north or south), but there is no way you could look east or west.

Day 123

Word of the Day:

spate (spat) (long a), sometimes *spait*

A. An overabundance
B. A sudden gush or outpouring (noun)
C. The past tense of spit
D. A heavy burden

Use: There was a *spate* of thunderous applause when she finished her performance.

Thought of the Day:

"Always be sure brain is in gear before engaging mouth" or put another way: "They never taste who always drink—they always talk who seldom think." *Anon*

Hook:

Farmer John has a pond (see illustration). In the pond there is a single lily pad that has the growth characteristic of doubling in size each night. If the pond will be full of lily pads on day 30, on what day will the pond be half full?

Solution:

Day 29. If the lily pad doubles in size each day, simply count backward, halving the size each day.

Day 124

Word of the Day:

de facto (de fak´ to)

A. Without basis in fact, groundless
B. Real or actual (adj.)
C. An equation incapable of being factored
D. False or unreal

Use: Her story, which was indeed *de facto*, sounded too incredible to be true.

Thought of the Day:

"It's going to be fun to see how long the meek can keep the earth after they inherit it." *Kin Hubbard*

Hook:

Remember Farmer John's pond from yesterday? It has a lily pad that doubles in size each day. Farmer John wants to take a short vacation, but he doesn't want to return and find his pond full of lily pads. So he decides to observe his pond for 20 days, and then make his decision about whether it will be safe to take his vacation. What do you suppose his decision will be?

Solution:

He'll probably decide it's okay to take his vacation. Draw the pond on the board (see illustration). Let the full pond represent day 30 (from yesterday). Divide the pond in two halves. One of those halves represents day 29. Now divide that in half, which represents day 28 and so forth. Work back to day 20. Amazing huh? It's called exponential growth (sure wish my bank account grew like that!).

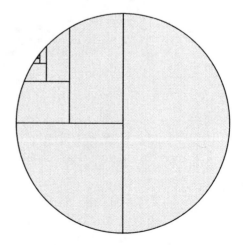

Day 125

Word of the Day:

stipend (sti´ pend) (long i)

A. An ornate kite
B. Rare, unusual
C. An enclosed area for small animals
D. An allowance or regular payment (noun)

Derivative: stipendiary
Use: As long as you are on this scholarship you will be receiving a monthly *stipend* to cover your academic expenses.

Thought of the Day:

"Happiness in life is not a destination, but rather a way to travel." *Anon*

Hook:

Tell this one as a funny story. Draw the following on the blackboard:

1 x 9 =
2 x 9 =
3 x 9 =
4 x 9 =
5 x 9 =
6 x 9 =
7 x 9 =
8 x 9 =
9 x 9 =
10 x 9 =

Tell the students that if they don't believe in luck (or coincidence) just watch what happened to one student. He was given the arithmetic quiz above. Not being very good at math and not having studied, the student knew he wasn't going to do very well. He studied the first problem and reasoned that one times anything is anything so the answer to the first problem must be nine (write in nine as the answer). He now looked through all the other problems and had no idea as to their answers. Getting to the last problem, he reasoned that he would multiply one number at a time, starting on the left: One times nine is nine (write it in) and then he remembered that the teacher had said that zero times anything is zero, so zero times nine must be zero (write in the zero). He now had the first and last problems finished, but still had no idea how to solve the others. Then he remembered what his father had taught him, *always size up the problem and know what you face*, so he

146

thought he would see how many more he had to do. He numbered the problems he had yet to do, starting with the second problem and working down (write these in) as below:

$1 \times 9 = 9$
$2 \times 9 = 1$
$3 \times 9 = 2$
$4 \times 9 = 3$
$5 \times 9 = 4$
$6 \times 9 = 5$
$7 \times 9 = 6$
$8 \times 9 = 7$
$9 \times 9 = 8$
$10 \times 9 = 90$

He now saw he had eight more problems to do, but it was hopeless, he had no idea how to do any of them. He reasoned, maybe it's not as bad as I thought, maybe I miscounted how many more I have to do. So he counted the unsolved problems again, this time starting from the bottom and coming up (write these in). You now have the following:

$1 \times 9 = 9$
$2 \times 9 = 18$
$3 \times 9 = 27$
$4 \times 9 = 36$
$5 \times 9 = 45$
$6 \times 9 = 54$
$7 \times 9 = 63$
$8 \times 9 = 72$
$9 \times 9 = 81$
$10 \times 9 = 90$

He still considered it hopeless because he had no idea how to do the math, so he decided to just hand it in the way it was. Lucky kid or what?

Day 126

Word of the Day:

plenary (plen´ er ree)

A. Complete or full (adj.)
B. Level, even
C. Smooth
D. Exceptional

Derivatives: plenarily, plenariness
Use: Since his powers as monarch were *plenary*, he often failed to consult his advisors before making a decision.

Thought of the Day:

"Do not follow the beaten path, but go instead where there is no path and leave a trail." *Anon*

Hook:

Here's one that is puzzling until you explain it or the students reason it out. Tell the students you are psychic. You are going to make a prediction. Write down your prediction on a piece of paper and put it in an envelope. Seal the envelope and give it to a student to hold. Here is how you make your prediction: Take the four digits of the current year and double them. If this is 2005 you have 4010. Add the number of students in the room—let us say there are 19. You now have 4029. Add today's date, the day only. Let us say today is the 17th. You now have 4046. This is the number you write as your prediction, keeping it a secret for the moment. You can now do the rest of the trick using a single student or you can have the entire class play along. Tell them you now want them to generate some random numbers (they will need pencil and paper or a calculator), but they are to do this silently, not letting you know any of the numbers they are generating. Have them write the year of their birth. Now under that, any past random year of their choice. Add those together. Now add to that total the number of students in the room today. Now let's go back to that random year. How many years ago was that? Add that to your running total. Now add today's date, the day only. Now add how old you will be at the end of this year. Tell them, "You now have a number and I know exactly what that number is. As a matter of fact, I knew what number you were going to pick even before we started." Have the student holding the envelope open it and show the number to the class. If they (and you) have done the math correctly, your number will match theirs.

Solution:

It's simple when you think about it. If you take your birth date and add your age, you have this year's date. If you take a random year and add how many years ago that was, you have this year's date. Together, those equal twice this year's date, as you used in your prediction. The other two, the number of students and today's date, are thrown into the sequence to make it seem as if the numbers are being randomly chosen. In fact you can substitute any other number for the number of students or today's date as long as they are numbers that you will know beforehand.

Day 127

Word of the Day:

obdurate (ob´ du rit)

A. Stubborn, inflexible (adj.)
B. Gifted
C. Slightly out of alignment
D. Oval in shape

Derivatives: obduracy, obdurately, obdurateness
Use: If Ben hadn't been so *obdurate*, he might have seen the weaknesses in his plan.

Thought of the Day:

"The opinion of the majority is not the final proof of what is right." *Schiller*

Hook:

Here are three more number/letter rebuses for students to decode:

1. 40 D and N of the GF

2. 3 P for a FG in F

3. 13 S in the AF

Solution:

1. 40 days and nights of the great flood

2. 3 points for a field goal in football

3. 13 stripes in the American flag

Day 128

Word of the Day:

flamboyant (flam boy´ yant)

(A.) Showy, with exaggerated style (adj.)
B. Able to float on water
C. A fiery type of Spanish music
D. Capable of catching fire

Derivatives: flamboyantly, flamboyance, flamboyancy
Use: Jean's *flamboyant* manner brought her lots of attention, not all of it good.

Thought of the Day:

"Leadership is a potent combination of strategy and character. However, if you must be without one, be without strategy." *Gen. Norman Schwarzkopf*

Hook:

This is a classic Chinese game played between two people. You can use matches, pennies, paper clips, checker pieces, or whatever else is handy. Arrange them as in the illustration below. Each player in turn removes as many as he or she likes from a horizontal row. The player who is forced to pick up the last object loses. Can you figure out a strategy to win?

Solution:

If you go first, remove one match from the bottom row. You can now control the play and be assured of winning. Even if you don't go first, if your opponent leaves any matches at all in all three rows, make your play to keep the two larger rows unequal by one. If your opponent takes the single match, play to keep the two remaining rows equal. Keep playing in this manner and eventually you will be able to win.

When they have mastered the first version, here is a second, more complex version. See if they can determine the strategy for winning in this version:

Thanks to Rebecca Scott for this version of the puzzle.

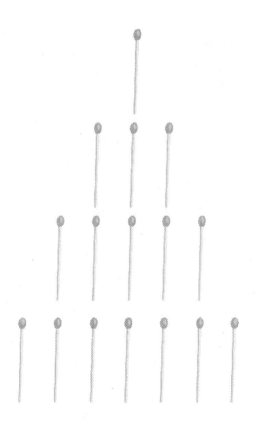

Day 129

Word of the Day:

salacious (sa lay´ shus)

A. Warmly welcoming, gracious
B. Critical and demeaning
C. Boring
D. Lewd, lustful (adj.)

Derivatives: salaciousness, salaciously, salacity
Use: The materials were not only suggestive, but *salacious* as well.

Thought of the Day:

"Life does not cease to be funny when people die any more than it ceases to be serious when they laugh." *G. B. Shaw*

Hook:

Another optical illusion to share with your students. Project or distribute the figure below.

Which line, top or bottom, on the right side of the figure is an extension of the line on the left?

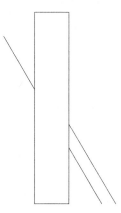

For a full-sized reproducible of this image, see Appendix, page 218.

Solution:

By now you have figured out that whatever it appears to be, it must be the opposite. Although the upper line is picked by most people, the lower line is actually the extension. Artists tell us that objects tend to settle or sink visually. In this case, the eye seems to rise slightly as it tries to track the line through the figure, making the figure sink and the line rise.

Day 130

Word of the Day:

pragmatic (prag mat´ ik)

A. Theoretical
B. Done by hand as opposed to machinery
C. Practical, realistic (adj.)
D. Foolish, silly

Derivatives: pragmatically, pragmatical, pragmatics, pragmatism
Use: The time for haggling about theoretical considerations is over, so let's get down to Earth and take a *pragmatic* approach to the problem.

Thought of the Day:

"It's been reasoned that the difference between genius and stupidity is that genius has limits." *Anon*

Hook:

"I live on an island," the man said, "and I'll give you a clue as to its location. Last Wednesday, my birthday, I was invited to two separate birthday parties in my honor, a few miles apart. Both were on Wednesday the 27th and both were at 3 p.m. Even though the parties were held miles apart, I attended each party from start to finish. Where do I live?" Can you figure it out?

Solution:

The man lives very close to the International Dateline in the Pacific Ocean. On Wednesday the 27th, he celebrated his birthday on one side of the line during one 24-hour period, then traveled across the line and repeated Wednesday the 27th all over again during the following 24-hour period. The only islands where such a situation can exist are the Solomon Islands in the South Pacific.

Day 131

Word of the Day:

détente (day taunt´)

A. Pertaining to daylight hours
B. Disgust
C. An easing of strained relations (noun)
D. Seeping slowly away

Use: After the prolonged and costly war, both sides were more than willing to engage in *détente*.

Thought of the Day:

"The injury we do and the one we suffer are not weighed on the same scale."
Aesop

Hook:

You have three cups and 10 marbles. Can you use all 10 marbles and all three cups and wind up with an odd number of marbles in each cup?

Hint:

You've got to think outside the box to get this one.

Solution:

Place five marbles in cup number 1, four marbles in cup number 2 and one marble in cup number 3. Now place cup number 3 into cup number 2. This is one of several ways to do it. See if your students can discover others.

Day 132

Word of the Day:

judicious (ju di´ shus)

A. Exercising sound judgment (adj.)
B. Lewd, crude, in poor taste
C. Possessing a tart or tangy flavor
D. With an intent to harm or injure

Derivatives: judiciousness, judiciously, judicial
Use: Marianne's *judicious* decisions early in the project assured success later on.

Thought of the Day:

"To fail is no crime—the crime is in aiming too low." *Lowell*

Hook:

Hope they like puns: An unsavory type decided to have his wife killed for the insurance. He contacted a hit man for the mob named Artie who explained that his going price for this sort of thing was ten thousand dollars. The husband agreed to the amount, but told Artie that he couldn't pay until he collected the insurance money.

Artie insisted on being paid at least a down payment, but the man, who insisted he was broke at the moment, pulled out his wallet and showed Artie that he had only a single dollar bill to his name.

Artie was not pleased, but after assurances from the man that the remainder would be forthcoming as soon as the insurance payment came through, he reluctantly took the dollar and agreed to do the dirty deed.

A few days later he followed the man's wife to the local Kroger grocery store and when found alone in the produce department, he strangled her. Unfortunately, the manager of the store stumbled onto the scene and, having seen Artie's face, the mobster had no choice but to strangle the store manager as well.

Fortunately, the whole thing was caught on the store's security cameras and Artie was arrested shortly thereafter. Can you guess what the newspaper headline was the next day?

Solution:

Artie Chokes Two For A Dollar At Kroger (Altogether now—*groan!*)

Day 133

Word of the Day:

insinuate (in sin´ u ate)

A. To act in an insincere manner
B. To pack tightly
C. To hint covertly (verb)
D. To resist temptation

Derivatives: insinuates, insinuated, insinuating
Use: Paul tried to *insinuate* that Jenny had cheated on the test.

Thought of the Day:

"A principle cannot be compromised, but only adhered to or surrendered. Honesty is abandoned by the theft of a dime as much as of a dollar." *Leonard*

Hook:

Inspector Davi steered the small powerboat next to the large freighter, the *Elgin Neff*, in the darkness of the harbor. The sound of the small craft's engine was drowned out by the sounds of the heavy diesel engines powering the winches and cranes as the crates of heavy machine parts were swung over from the dock and lowered onto the deck.

The inspector had received information that something illegal was going on concerning the cargo, but he had observed the ship all morning through high power binoculars and had seen nothing out of the ordinary other than a small private power boat that had recklessly sped through the harbor and hit the freighter a glancing blow, doing no real damage but leaving a long streak of red paint along the freighter's side near the water line. The captain of the freighter had twice gone ashore, both times returning within minutes. The tattered Norwegian flag had been fluttering in the stiff breeze, and once, the inspector had noticed some technicians repairing the radar mast. However, none of these things in itself was cause to detain the ship that was scheduled to sail tomorrow.

As his small craft bumped the hull of the ship slightly, Inspector Davi flicked on his flashlight for just a moment. Yes, there it was, the same red streak of paint he had seen this morning left by the careless boater. This was indeed the ship he was looking for. Quietly he made his way around the ship, noting the work going on of loading the crates labeled **HEAVY MACHINE PARTS** and the crew going about their other shipboard duties. He noted that three technicians were again working on the shipboard radar mast. Satisfied, he returned quietly to shore and telephoned the harbor patrol.

"I want the *Elgin Neff* detained for inspection," he said to the harbor patrol chief. "There is definitely something amiss aboard that ship." What has made Inspector Davi suspicious?

Solution:

What alerted the inspector was that while he had noted the small power boat scrape paint onto the hull of the freighter that morning, the paint scrape was still visible above the water line even though what should have been heavy crates had been loaded onto the ship all day. That much heavy cargo would have made the ship settle in the water and the paint scrape should have been below the water line by now. Yet, it was still visible, indicating that something suspicious is going on with the cargo being loaded.

Day 134

Word of the Day:

sloop (slup) (long u)

A. A lazy person, a bum
B. A single-masted sailing boat
C. A stew made from leftovers
D. To move under cover of darkness

Use: Her prow splitting the water, the racing *sloop* tacked hard into the wind.

Thought of the Day:

"It is important that students bring a certain ragamuffin, barefoot irreverence to their studies. They are not here to worship what is known, but to question it." *Jacob Bronowski*

Hook:

Six pennies are closely packed as in the parallelogram array below (at left). Your task is to slide pennies, one at a time, to new positions and end with the circular pattern (at right). The circle must be precise and not just *eyeballed*. To do this you must slide each coin so it touches two other coins that rigidly determine its position. Sliding a coin and repositioning it is one move. What is the lowest number of moves required?

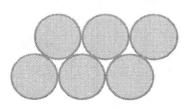
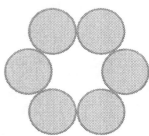

Solution:

3 moves.
1. Slide coin 6 to touch 4 and 5 from below
2. Slide coin 5 to touch 2 and 3 from below (where 6 used to be)
3. Slide coin 3 to touch 5 and 6

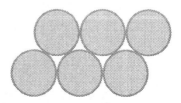

Day 135

Word of the Day:

microcosm (my´ cro ka zum)

A. A little world
B. A small parasite that lives in the digestive tract of pigs
C. A medical instrument
D. A measurement of distance (metric)

Derivatives: microcosmic, microcosmically
Use: Michelle was shocked at how trivial popularity really was once she left her high school *microcosm*.

Thought of the Day:

"It is with our passions as it is with fire and water; they are good servants but very bad masters." *L'estrange*

Hook:

This riddle, one of the oldest known, is still good for generating some disagreement:

A man, while looking at a portrait, is asked whose picture it is. He replies, "Brothers and sisters have I none, but that man's father is my father's son." At whose picture is the man looking?

Solution:

The portrait is of the man's son. Many mistakenly argue that the man is looking at a picture of himself. If he had said, "that man is my father's son," then that solution would be correct. But what he said was, "that man's *father* is my father's son." Another way to avoid the confusion is to substitute the word *me* for the cumbersome phrase, *my father's son*. Then the statement becomes, *that man's father is me*.

Day 136

Word of the Day:

ocarina (auk´ a ree´ na)

A. A folk dance of the Slav Republic
B. A circular stage with the audience seated on all sides
C. A small-ovoid shaped flute (noun)
D. A public square

Use: When the musical group added the *ocarina* to their instrumentation, it gave an authentic sound to the folk tune.

Thought of the Day:

"The ripest peach is usually on the highest limb of the tree." *James Whitcomb Riley*

Hook:

What comes next in the series?

F28 M31 A30 M31

Hint:

It's not mathematical.

Solution:

J30. (February has 28 days, March 31, etc.)

Day137

Word of the Day:

wench (winch)

- (A.) A young woman (noun)
- B.   To strain abnormally
- C.   A device for rolling cable
- D.   A motorized raft

Use: With a fetching smile, the winsome *wench* brought our drinks to the table.

Thought of the Day:

"There is no greater disloyalty to the great pioneers of human progress than to refuse to budge an inch from where they stood." *W. R. Inge*

Hook:

What do these words have in common?

1. Race car

2. Kayak

3. Level

Solution:

They are palindromes. They are the same whether read left to right or right to left.

Day 138

Word of the Day:

heretic (hair´ e tik)

(A.) A dissenter, one who defies conventional belief (noun)
B. An outlaw or criminal
C. A philosopher
D. A decorative stitch in quilting

Derivatives: heretical, heretically, heresy

Use: Although nonconformity is still frowned upon, at least today you don't have to be worried about being burned at the stake for being a *heretic.*

Thought of the Day:

"Gold is tried by fire, bravery by adversity." *Seneca*

Hook:

Here are three more paraphrased titles for the students to decode:

1. Chiroptera abiding in a steepled bell tower.

2. Luminescence of the shiny metallic element, atomic number 79; swinging entrance structure; span.

3. 15th state of the union horse race of 3-year-olds on the first Saturday in May.

Solution:

1. Bats in the belfry

2. Golden Gate Bridge

3. Kentucky Derby

Day 139

Word of the Day:

sanguine (sang´ gwin)

A. The color of blood (adj.)
B. At ease, peaceful
C. A Spanish wine
D. Passionate, with deep feeling

Derivatives: sanguinely, sanguineness, sanguinity, sanguineous, sanguinolent, sanguinary, sanguinarily
Use: The brilliant *sanguine* sunset filled us all with a sense of awe.

Thought of the Day:

"Books are the true levelers. They give to all, who will faithfully use them, the society, the spiritual presence, of the best and greatest of our races." *W. E. Channing*

Hook:

You have two partially inflated balloons connected via a glass tube with a valve shutting off the tube (as illustrated). When the valve is opened what will happen?

A. Nothing

B. The small balloon will expand at the expense of the larger

C. The large balloon will expand at the expense of the smaller

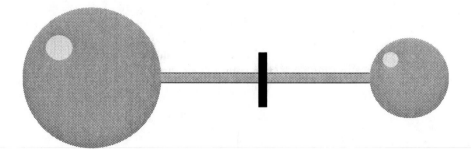

Solution:

C. Oddly enough the small balloon has more internal pressure so its air will be forced into the larger balloon. Remember how hard it is to start to inflate a balloon, but once it is started how much easier it is to inflate the rest of the way?

Day 140

Word of the Day:

taciturn (tass´ i turn)

A. Having little or nothing to say (adj.)
B. Out of sync, inharmonious
C. An instrument for determining G forces
D. The dramatic climax of a play or motion picture

Derivatives: taciturnly, taciturnity, tacit, tacitly, tacitness
Use: Due to his *taciturn* nature, it was hard to tell where he stood on the issue.

Thought of the Day:

"Originality does not consist in saying what no one has ever said before, but in saying exactly what you yourself think." *Anon*

Hook:

Double Your Money is a good trick you can do with just a modicum of practice. Before class, arrange a napkin or handkerchief on the table in a somewhat crumpled manner with a quarter hidden under one corner. After the class is seated, pick up the corner of the napkin with the quarter hidden in the folds, holding the corner of the napkin and quarter hidden against the fingers by your thumb. You now whip the napkin to show it is *empty*. Now grab the other end of the napkin in the left hand and by flipping your hands away from you, create a rolled napkin. Tell a student that if he or she will loan you a quarter, you will double the money in only moments. Have the student place the donated quarter in the middle of the rolled up napkin. Lift the two ends up to tie them in a knot. As you lift the ends together, release the hidden coin into the rolled up napkin where it will slide down to the middle of the roll. Tie the ends and you secretly have both quarters tied into the rolled up napkin. Wave your magic wand or whatever and have the student untie and unroll the napkin above the table top. When the student unties the knot his or her original quarter will fall to the table. Encourage him or her to continue unrolling the napkin. As he or she does so, the hidden coin will fall to the table.

"And there is your interest," you say, letting the student pocket both quarters (or not, if finances are a little tight this month).

Day 141

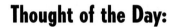

Word of the Day:

undulation (un du lay´ shun)

A. That which has not been earned
B. A repetitive rising and falling movement (noun)
C. Loud applause
D. An unspecified period of time

Derivatives: undulate, undulated, undulates
Use: The constant *undulation* of the boat was making us all seasick.

Thought of the Day:

"So long as you are praised, you can be sure that you are not yet on your own path—but on someone else's." *Nietzsche*

Hook:

June has a box in which there are 6 blue gum balls, 4 red gum balls, and 2 white gum balls. The box is on a high shelf where she can reach into the box, but is not able to see what color candy she is grabbing. Three of her friends have just arrived and all of them insist they each want the same color gum ball. How many gum balls will she have to grab from the box to *ensure* she can give each of her friends the same color?

Hint:

Think worst case scenario.

Solution:

Seven. The worst case would be that she would draw the 2 white gum balls, 2 red gum balls, and 2 blue gum balls for a total of 6 gum balls. The seventh ball drawn would have to match either blue or red.

Day 142

Word of the Day:

Yiddish (yid´ ish)

A. A plum pudding
B. Shy, backward
C. Hebrew language (noun)
D. Anxious, nervous

Use: His mile-a-minute *Yiddish* left us all struggling to understand what he had said.

Thought of the Day:

"If you call a tail a leg, how many legs does a dog have? Five? No, calling a tail a leg doesn't make it so." *Abraham Lincoln*

Hook:

See if the kids can come up with a logical explanation for the following: A man is tried for the crime of murder and found guilty. The judge says, "This is the strangest case I have ever seen. You are, without doubt, guilty, yet the law requires me to set you free." What is the reason for the judge's decision?

Solution:

The man was one of a pair of Siamese twins.

Day 143

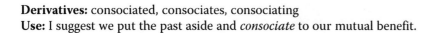

Word of the Day:

consociate (con so´ she ate)

A. To disagree on principle
B. To become angry
C. To join in friendship (verb)
D. To dance

Derivatives: consociated, consociates, consociating
Use: I suggest we put the past aside and *consociate* to our mutual benefit.

Thought of the Day:

"Everyone is a damn (darn) fool for at least five minutes every day. Wisdom consists in not exceeding the limit." *Elbert Hubbard*

Hook:

Here's a toughie. What unique characterisitc do the following words have in common?

MONTH, ORANGE, SILVER, PURPLE

Solution:

No word in the English language rhymes with them.

Day 144

Word of the Day:

imprudent (im pru´ dent)

A. Impolite
B. Ineffective, useless
C. Unwise, rash (adj.)
D. With absolute confidence

Derivatives: imprudence, imprudent
Use: You are being *imprudent* if you think rushing to judgment will solve the problem.

Thought of the Day:

"When all is said and done, a lot more is said than done." *Anon*

Hook:

Let's see if your students can decode this rebus:

Solution:

I've been framed.

Day 145

Word of the Day:

hierarchy (hire´ ar kee)

(A.) Classification in order of sequence, rank, or importance (noun)
B. Royal or imperial family
C. Employment practices of a business or organization
D. A team with a distinguished record of achievement

Derivatives: hierarchies, hierarch, hierarchism, hierarchist, hierarchical, hierarchic, hierarchically
Use: His job as mail clerk placed him on the lowest rung of the office *hierarchy*.

Thought of the Day:

"A prudent question is one half of wisdom." *William James*

Hook:

Your kid brother wants to sail his toy sailboat. The problem is there is absolutely no wind. So, you get an idea. You take a battery operated fan, attach it to the stern of the boat, and let the wind blow into the sail (see illustration). Will it work?

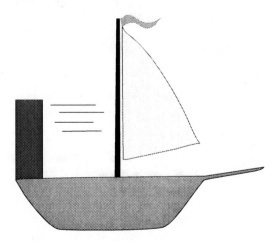

Solution:

No way. Remember that guy Newton and his law of action and reaction? The boat will actually be propelled *backwards*. The sail cannot capture all the wind generated by the fan and the opposite reaction of the fan will actually make the boat move slightly backwards.

Day 146

Word of the Day:

sinewy (sin´ u ee)

A. Sinful
B. Lean and muscular (adj.)
C. Made up of multiple parts
D. A Native American language of the Sinew tribe of northern Oregon

Use: The muscles in his *sinewy* frame rippled as he carried his surf board to the water's edge.

Thought of the Day:

"He who thinks he can do without others is sadly mistaken, but he who thinks others cannot do without him is even more so." *La Rochefoucauld*

Hook:

Three business men, Smith, a lawyer, Jones, an accountant, and Giles, a realtor, live in the same area. Coincidentally three employees of the local sports arena have the same last names. The accountant and the ticket seller live in Morehead. The Realtor and the lighting technician live in Salt Lick, while the lawyer and the concessions manager live in Farmers between Morehead and Salt Lick. The ticket seller's namesake earns $40,000 a year and the concessions manager earns exactly one-third that of the businessman living nearest to him. Finally, the sports arena employee Smith is single, while the lighting technician is married.

What is the name of the concessions manager?

Solution:

The ticket seller cannot be Smith, because Smith the lawyer is the concessions manager's nearest neighbor and his income is exactly divisible by three ($40,000 is not). Also, the lighting technician cannot be Smith because Smith is single and the lighting technician is married. Ergo: Smith is the concessions manager.

Day 147

Word of the Day:

scepter (sep´ ter)

- (A.) A decorative ceremonial staff or baton (noun)
- B. A thief
- C. A spy or informant
- D. A medical instrument for removing the outer layer of skin

Derivatives: sceptering, sceptered, scepters
Use: Holding his *scepter* high, the grand marshall began leading the graduation processional.

Thought of the Day:

"It is observation, not old age, which brings wisdom." *Anon*

Hook:

Imagine two bridges that are alike in every respect except that every dimension of one is twice that of the other. For instance, the larger bridge is twice as long, twice as wide, its structural members twice as thick, etc. Which bridge is stronger or is their strength the same?

Solution:

The smaller bridge is much stronger. If a steel girder in the larger bridge is twice the size, in every dimension, of one in the smaller bridge, it will be twice as strong but weigh eight times as much. The double-sized bridge would probably be so weak that it would collapse under its own weight.

Day 148

Word of the Day:

vehement (ve´ a mint)

A. With hatred
B. Pertaining to movement
C. A mound of dirt piled up for defense
D. Emphatic, with vigor (adj.)

Derivatives: vehemence, vehemency, vehemently
Use: Everyone took note of John's argument, especially when he was so *vehement* in his presentation.

Thought of the Day:

"Throughout history the most debilitating human ailment has always been cold feet." *Anon*

Hook:

What plural masculine word becomes singular feminine when you add an S?

Solution:

Princes becomes *princess*.

Day 149

Word of the Day:

unseemly (un seem´ lee)

A. Untrue, illegitimate
B. Unbecoming, in poor taste (adj.)
C. Without support
D. Unclear, murky

Derivatives: unseemlier, unseemliest, unseemliness
Use: The man's *unseemly* behavior in the restaurant embarrassed his wife and children.

Thought of the Day:

"Contradiction is not a sign of falsity, nor is the lack of contradiction a sign of truth." *Pascal*

Hook:

The king has 10 horses. He has only nine royal stalls however (see below). The king insists that each of 10 horses has a stall to itself, that the stalls not be altered in any way, and that the horses are to remain unharmed. No horse is pregnant. Even the royal mathematician was stumped until a quick witted stable boy was able to fit 10 horses into the nine stalls. Can you?

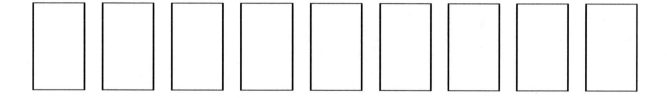

Solution

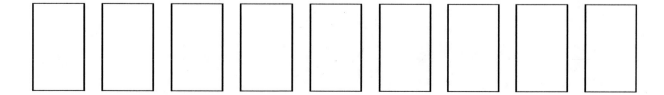

Day 150

Word of the Day:

blackguard (blag´ erd)

A. A royal guardsman
B. A hobo, bum
C. A scoundrel (noun)
D. A board game dating from the 15th century

Derivatives: blackguarded, blackguarding, blackguards, blackguardism, blackguardly
Use: Shamelessly preying on unsuspecting women, the *blackguard* seemed to possess no conscience at all.

Thought of the Day:

"Have you ever noticed that nature absolutely delights in punishing stupid people?" *Anon*

Hook:

Three couples went to a garden together. The girls each picked a flower of a different color. One picked red, one yellow, and one blue. The boys each also picked flowers of the same three colors, but when the boy with the red flower saw the girl with the yellow flower, who was with another boy, he commented that no boy and girl were paired with someone who held the same color flower.

Question:

What color flower does the boy have who is paired with the girl who picked a red flower?

Solution:

The boy with the red flower must be with the girl who has a blue flower. She cannot have red because then their flower colors would match, and she can't be yellow because the boy with the red flower saw the girl with the yellow flower paired with another boy. Using the same reasoning, the girl with the yellow flower can't be with either the boy with a blue flower or the boy with the yellow flower. Process of elimination leaves the girl with the red flower paired with the boy with the yellow flower.

Day 151

Word of the Day:

hauteur (ho tur´)

A. A hat box
B. Arrogance (noun)
C. A doorman
D. A small piece of luggage used to carry toiletries

Use: His *hauteur* was especially evident when he showed that superior, self-confident smile.

Thought of the Day:

"The battle is not to the strong alone, but rather to the vigilant, the active, and the brave." *Patrick Henry*

Hook:

Three more number/word rebuses to decode:

1. 12 S of the Z

2. 1 W on a U

3. 200 D for PG in M

Solution:

1. 12 signs of the zodiac

2. 1 wheel on a unicycle

3. 200 dollars for passing go in Monopoly

Day 152

Word of the Day:

unduly (un dew´ lee)

A. Ugly, unattractive
(B.) Without justification (adj.)
C. Irresponsible
D. Informal

Use: She was *unduly* accused of taking the purse from Kathleen's locker.

Thought of the Day:

"Advice is seldom welcome, and those who need it most always like and heed it least." *Lord Chesterfield*

Hook:

Here's another interesting optical illusion. Duplicate or project it and ask the students if the horizontal lines are parallel. Do they run straight across the page or do they slant? Try using a straightedge.

For a full-size reproducible of this image, see Appendix, page 219.

Weird, eh?

Day 153

Word of the Day:

vaunted (von´ ted)

A. Boastful (adj.)
B. Brave
C. Loyal
D. Legendary

Derivatives: vaunt, vaunting, vaunts, vaunter, vauntingly
Use: The *vaunted* Tigers, undefeated throughout the season, were humbled by a 28-0 thrashing at the hands of the lowly Lions.

Thought of the Day:

"We fear before we hate and we fear that which we do not understand. A child who does not understand, fears, and that child grows to become an adult who hates." *Anon*

Hook:

The Eiffel Tower was completed in 1889 and remains one of the artistic and engineering marvels of the world. How tall is it? It is 492 feet plus half its own height. Can you figure it out?

Solution:

984 feet. If 492 plus half equals something, then the 492 must be the other half. You don't really need to use algebra but . . .

$492 + .5X = X$

$492 = .5X$

$984 = X$

Day 154

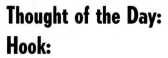

Word of the Day:

esurient (e sur´ ee ent)

A. Hungry or greedy (adj.)
B. Depressed
C. Short tempered
D. Impolite

Derivatives: esurience, esuriency, esuriently

Use: The man's conviction didn't seem to satisfy the *esurient* district attorney, who pressed for the death penalty.

Thought of the Day:

"Imagination is more important than knowledge." *Albert Einstein*

Hook:

Here's a neat card trick that requires a minimum amount of practice. Fan the cards face down and have a student pick a card. Tell the student to memorize it and show it to the other students. Turn your back (this is all done with the cards face down). Cut the deck. Holding half the deck in the left and the remainder in the right hand, slide the top card in the left hand back toward you just a bit so it is slightly misaligned with the other cards, but not so much as to be noticeable. Now turn back around and have the student place the card on top of those in your left hand. The card is now on top of the misaligned card. Place the rest of the deck from your right hand on top of the student's card and holding the cards toward the students, tap the end of the deck away from you (you are seeming to align the deck, but the misaligned card is still sticking out the back toward you where the students can't see it). Now cut the deck at the misaligned card. This puts the student's card on the bottom of the pile in your right hand. Now shuffle (either an overhand cut shuffle or a riffle shuffle), but be sure that you keep the student's card at the bottom (practice a time or two and you'll find it isn't very hard to do). You can shuffle as many times as you want (you may even use both shuffles to give the student's the impression you are really mixing up the cards) as long as you keep the target card at the bottom of the deck.

Now tell the students that *you* are not going to find the card but that the *student* will. Hold the deck in your right hand with the first, second, and third fingers underneath against the target card and the thumb on top, using only moderate pressure. Now have the student use his or her first and second fingers together to whack down on the deck (the objective is to spill the cards from your hand). Your fingers underneath are creating enough friction that the target card will stay put while the others tumble onto the floor. If there are additional cards left in your hand after the first whack, have the student whack them again until only one card is left. Before you turn it over, have the student say aloud what card was drawn, then dramatically turn the card over and voilà, magically it's that card! David Copperfield, eat your heart out!

Day 155

Word of the Day:

tangible (tan´ ji bul)

A. Real and capable of being touched (adj.)
B. Tart, sour
C. Rounded or smoothed on one end
D. Waterproof

Derivatives: tangibility, tangibleness, tangibly

Use: The hatred was so strong between them, the acrimony was almost *tangible* when they were in the same room.

Thought of the Day:

"It is with life as with the play—it matters not how long the action is spun out, but how good the action is." *Seneca*

Hook:

A little humor to start the day: A researcher had discovered that when the chicks of coastal aquatic birds were fed to dolphins, the dolphins could be kept alive indefinitely. Only the very youngest of the chicks would do, however, and they were hard to get. There was a nearby wildlife sanctuary, but not only was it guarded by a fence, there was a large, African carnivorous feline roaming free as well. Having exhausted his supply of chicks, however, the researcher became desperate enough that he decided to sneak into the sanctuary that night. To quiet the huge cat he laced some raw meat with a potent tranquilizer and threw the meat across the fence, where it was quickly eaten by the ravenous beast that was soon sleeping soundly. He climbed the fence, stepped over the sleeping cat, robbed several nests of their chicks, stepped back across the African cat and made his escape. But he was soon captured and thrown in jail to await trial. The charge?

Transporting underage gulls across a staid lion for immortal porpoises.

Day 156

Word of the Day:

jibe (gibe) (long i)

A. A fruit drink of Bermuda
B. A signal flag or series of flags
C. The metal loop through which a belt passes for fastening
D. To be in agreement or harmony (verb)

Derivatives: jibed, jibing, jibes
Use: The man's story did not *jibe* with the facts.

Thought of the Day:

"The two hardest things to handle in life are failure—and success." *Anon*

Hook:

Inspector Davi looked over the refreshment table in the ballroom of the mansion where 27 of 28 people had died of poisoning.

"Was there a food common to them all?" he asked the servant.

"Yes sir. They all had the canapés, but so did Mr. Jensen, who not only survived, but shows no sign of illness at all."

"Hmmmm," mused the inspector. "Mr. Jensen, did you use a napkin with your canapés as did the others?"

"Why, yes I did," answered the man.

"Then perhaps we should look elsewhere. What about the punch?" he asked, noting the bright red drink and few remaining ice cubes in the large serving bowl.

"Sir, they all drank from the punch bowl, including Mr. Jensen," replied the servant.

"Yes, I had a quick drink of punch as soon as they brought it in, ate a bite, and left. My wife was due in on the 9:15 so I excused myself early and left to meet her."

"Ah ha!" said the inspector, "perhaps the bowl of punch was poisoned after you left."

"Oh, no sir," replied the servant, "I served the punch and I can attest to the fact that no one tampered with the punch after Mr. Jensen left."

"This case will bear more looking into," observed Davi, "but at least I know now how the poison was administered."

What has inspector Davi deduced?

Solution:

Since the only commonalities were the food and drink, and the food had been ruled out, he surmised that the punch must have been poisoned. But how could Jensen have drunk the punch and not been affected? Obviously the poison was not yet in the punch. The inspector reasoned that the ice cubes that were poured into the punch bowl to keep the punch cool just before serving held the poison. Jensen was unaffected since he drank immediately after the punch was served and before the ice cubes had melted, releasing the poison.

Day 157

Word of the Day:

venerable (ven´ er a bul)

A. Worthy of respect (adj.)
B. Hated, despised
C. Airy, well ventilated
D. Easily fooled

Derivatives: venerableness, venerability, venerably, venerate, veneration
Use: The *venerable* senior senator entered the chamber to the hushed respect of both sides of the aisle.

Thought of the Day:

"The very purpose of our existence is to reconcile the glowing opinion we hold of ourselves with the appalling things that others think about us." *Quentin Crisp*

Hook:

This inductive game is called *In a Perfect World*. You start the game, then each student tries to figure out the pattern by responding. You give that student feedback as to the correctness or incorrectness of the response, and it moves to the next student who does the same. This may take several rounds for the students to figure out, so you may want to limit it to one round per day until they have solved the pattern.

You explain to the students that you will start by saying, "In a perfect world there will be _____ but no _____." Each student in turn will make the same statement filling in the blanks with his or her own words. You will tell them whether they are correct or not, and then move on to the next student until all have played. They are to try to figure out the pattern from the responses and your feedback. As soon as they figure it out, they should start responding correctly each time it is their turn until all the students have figured it out.

Now to start the game. The pattern is that the first blank is filled with a word that has double letters, the second blank with a word which does not contain double letters. So you might start by saying, "In a perfect world there would be puppies, but no dogs." Then it becomes the first student's turn. If the student fills the first blank with a word with a double letter and the second with a word without a double letter you give a "correct" response and move on. If neither or only one blank is correctly filled, you give an "incorrect" response and move on to the next student. The responses do not have to be logical and in fact some of the students may start giving some zany answers, which makes for lots of fun. Remind them periodically that they are trying to find the pattern and to listen carefully to the responses and to your feedback. You can play variations of the game by using other patterns. Instead of a word with a double letter, you might use the pattern of both words having an A in them, etc. You may even wish to let the students pick some of the patterns and try to stump the class.

Day 158

Word of the Day:

rufescent (ru fes´ ant)

A. Blistering
B. Tinged with red (adj.)
C. Sorrowful
D. Full of energy

Derivative: rufescence
Use: We watched the horrifying shark attack, dumbfounded as the water became *rufescent* with the blood of the victim.

Thought of the Day:

"Victory goes to the player or team who makes the *next to last* mistake."
Savielly Tartakower

Hook:

Two new titles or phrases for charades: Remember, no talking, pantomime only, and a 1 minute time limit.

1. *Lord of the Rings*

2. The early bird gets the worm

Day 159

Word of the Day:

rancor (rang´ kor)

(A.) Ill will (noun)
B. Sleepiness
C. Isolation
D. Suicidal

Derivatives: rancorously, rancorousness
Use: Because of the long standing *rancor* between them, reaching an agreement was out of the question.

Thought of the Day:

"We make a living by what we get, but we make a life by what we give."
Winston Churchill

Hook:

See if they can figure out this one:

"Amanda has over a hundred CDs," said Bill

"No, I'm sure she has fewer than that," replied Anne.

"All I can say for sure is that Amanda has at least one CD," stated Zach.

If only one of these statements is true, how many CDs does Amanda have?

Solution:

The three possibilities are TFF, FTF, FFT (since only one statement is true). Of the three, the only combination that does not lead to a contradiction is FTF. Ergo: Amanda has no CDs at all.

Day 160

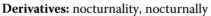

Word of the Day:

nocturnal (nok tur´ nal)

A. An orchestral composition
B. Nonsensical, irrational
C. Pertaining to night (adj.)
D. A painting depicting a rural or pastoral scene

Derivatives: nocturnality, nocturnally
Use: The crickets began chirping, adding their song to the *nocturnal* symphony.

Thought of the Day:

"The real voyage of discovery consists not in seeking new landscapes but in seeing with new eyes." *Marcel Proust*

Hook:

An anagram is a word or phrase, the letters of which can be rearranged to form a new word or phrase. See if your students can rearrange the following words into one word anagrams.

1. Easter egg

2. Remote

3. There we sat

Solution:

1. Segregate

2. Meteor

3. Sweetheart

Day 161

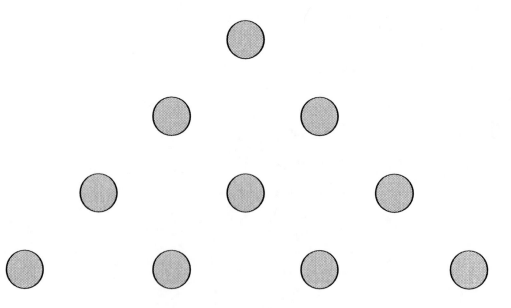

Word of the Day:

lazaretto (laz a ret´ o)

A. A tiled multi-colored patio
B. A direction in music meaning to be played at a steady, slow pace.
C. A hospital for patients with contagious diseases (noun)
D. A European coffee house

Use: The doctor's previous work at a *lazaretto* enabled him to diagnose the leprosy almost immediately.

Thought of the Day:

"The best rose bush, after all, is not that with the fewest thorns, but that which bears the finest flowers." *Henry Van Dyke*

Hook:

Rearrange only three of the coins to make the triangle point downward.

Solution:

Move 7 and 10 upward so they form a horizontal line with 2 and 3. Move 1 around and down so that it is below and between 8 and 9.

Day 162

Word of the Day:

rejoinder (re join´ der)

(A.) An answer or reply (noun)
B. A woodworking tool for smoothing the edges of boards
C. A person returning from a long voyage or trip
D. The cog of a gear

Derivative: rejoin
Use: Angered by the man's rudeness, Mike's *rejoinder* was curt and biting.

Thought of the Day:

"The trouble with joining the rat race is that even if you win you're still a rat."
Lily Tomlin

Hook:

There are three sets of paired words below. Both the paired words belong to the same category and both can be completed by inserting the same three letter sequence (a different three letter sequence for each pair). See if your students can figure them out.

1. SWE_ _ _   _ _ _MARK

2. _ _ _SS   _ _ _CKERS

3. _ _ _CH   _ _ _R

Solution:

1. SWE<u>DEN</u> DEN<u>MARK</u> (Countries)

2. <u>CHE</u>SS <u>CHE</u>CKERS (Games)

3. <u>PEA</u>CH <u>PEA</u>R (Fruits)

Day 163

Word of the Day:

precipice (press´ i pus)

A. The edge of a cliff or any dangerous situation (noun)
B. An important message
C. Highly pertinent and to the point
D. No longer needed, already accomplished

Use: He dared not stand too close to the *precipice* lest he lose his footing in the soft rain soaked earth and plunge to his death.

Thought of the Day:

"The purpose of life is a life of purpose." *Robert Byrne*

Hook:

See if they can answer this one.

What 11-letter word do almost all Americans spell incorrectly?

Solution:

Incorrectly (gotcha!)

Day 164

Word of the Day:

incumbent (in cum´ bent)

(A.) Obligation or dependence upon (adj.)
B. Repetitive
(C.) Current officeholder (noun/adj.)
D. With hesitation

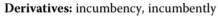

Derivatives: incumbency, incumbently
Use #1: With no one else to help, it became *incumbent* upon me to finish the job. (adj.)
Use #2: The *incumbent* is heavily favored in the election. (noun)
Use #3: The *incumbent* governor has left a lasting mark on state politics. (adj.)

Thought of the Day:

"Our increase in knowledge is comparable to the man who, wanting to know more about the moon, climbs onto the roof of his house for a closer look."
Albert Einstein

Hook:

A man lives on the 20th floor of a high-rise apartment building. Every weekday morning he gets in the elevator, rides to the ground floor and goes to work. Every weekday evening, arriving from work, he gets into the elevator and, if there is another passenger, rides to the 20th floor. If he is alone however, he rides to the 16th floor, gets off and walks the last four flights of stairs to his apartment. That is, unless the weather is rainy, in which case he rides directly to the 20th floor whether there is another person on the elevator or not. What could explain the man's behavior?

Solution:

The man is a dwarf. When he rides down, he can easily reach the ground floor button. When he rides up however, he can only reach as far as the 16th floor button. If there is someone else on the elevator, he asks that person to push the 20th floor button, or if it has been raining and he is carrying an umbrella, he can use the umbrella and its tip to push the button.

Day 165

Word of the Day:

junket (junk´ it)

(A.) A trip or tour (noun)
B. A small boat with a single sail
C. A disorganized mess
D. A brightly colored parrot of South America

Derivatives: junketed, junketing, junkets
Use: The congressional overseas *junket* was primarily a fact-finding tour.

Thought of the Day:

"Being unable to make what is just, strong, we have made what is strong, just." *Pascal*

Hook:

Whip the Knot is a trick done with a cloth napkin, handkerchief, or any piece of soft cloth material of about the same size. Beforehand, secretly tie a knot in one end of the napkin and hide it out of sight. Make sure the students don't see it ahead of time. With the class seated, reach down out of sight grasping the knot between the thumb and last three fingers and pulling it into sight so that the back of your hand is toward the students. This hides the knot in your hand and appears to the students to be an ordinary napkin. Give them some patter about being able to tie a knot in the napkin with one hand. Now raise the unknotted end up with your left hand and grasp it lightly between the third and fourth finger of the right hand, again hidden from the students. Now shake your hand downward as if cracking a whip. Keep the knot firmly secured as you let the unknotted end release. Hold up the napkin as before and say something to the effect that you had better try again. Do the same thing again and even a third time, each time snapping the napkin but *failing* to tie the knot. Now bring the unknotted end up a final time, holding both ends in your hand. Mention that you forgot the pixie dust or some other nonsense, and reach out into empty air with the left hand pretending to wave the pixie dust at the right hand, which still holds the two ends. At the very moment that the students' attention is diverted to the waving left hand, release the knotted end from your hand. It will appear the napkin has magically knotted itself.

Day 166

Word of the Day:

maître d'hôtel (may´ tra do tel´) (long o) or *maître d'*
(may´ tra d´)

- A. A mother figure
- B. A service elevator
- C. The head waiter in a restaurant (noun)
- D. A French army officer, equivalent to an
  American major

Use: The *maître d'* checked the list again but our reservations were nowhere to be found.

Thought of the Day:

"The good Lord never gives you more than you can handle—unless you die of something." *Anon*

Hook:

Here are three more paraphrased titles for the students to decode:

1. Nocturnal time span of unbroken quiet.

2. Solitary Texas law enforcement official.

3. Distant sun martial hostilities.

Solution:

1. "Silent Night"

2. "The Lone Ranger"

3. *Star Wars*

Day 167

Word of the Day:

lacuna (la cu´ na)

A. An ocean fish of the perch family
B. Crazy, insane
C. A mountain goat of Peru and Chile
D. An empty space or gap (noun)

Derivatives: lacunal, lacunar, lacunary
Use: Closer inspection revealed a *lacuna* where a cog had broken off the gear wheel.

Thought of the Day:

"When ideas fail, words come in very handy." *Goethe*

Hook:

A large truck containing hundreds of uncaged parakeets approaches a bridge. The sign at the bridge indicates the maximum weight the bridge can safely hold. The truck is slightly less than the maximum, but when the weight of the parakeets is added, the truck and parakeets together slightly exceed the maximum. Is there a means of getting the truck across the bridge without exceeding the maximum weight?

Solution:

Not unless you leave something behind (part of the truck or some of the birds or yourself). The idea of striking the side of the truck and keeping the birds in flight as the truck crosses the bridge is erroneous. The truck is a closed system so the total weight is the truck and birds—period. The birds in flight will create their weight in downward flapping pressure—thus there would be no decrease in overall weight (and banging on the truck also annoys the birds).

Day 168

Word of the Day:

nidify (nid'-i-fi)

A.   To trivialize
B.   To make null and void
C.   To build a nest (verb)
D.   To reduce in size

Derivatives: nidified, nidifying, nidifies, nidificate, nidificant, nidification
Usage: We watched the tiny spider spin and spin, oblivious to everything as it continued to *nidify* industriously.

Thought of the Day:

"Take note that the Spartans never asked how many the enemy numbered but only where they were to be found." *Anon*

Hook:

See if your kids can decode this rebus:

OPINION OPINIOn

Solution:

A slight difference of opinion.

Day 169

Word of the Day:

egregious (e gree´ jus)

A. Based upon religious principles
B. Agreeable
C. Timely
D. Exceptionally bad (adj.)

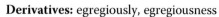

Derivatives: egregiously, egregiousness
Use: His behavior was so *egregious* that several members of the committee left the meeting in protest.

Thought of the Day:

"To profit from good advice requires more wisdom than to give it." *J. C. Collins*

Hook:

Your task is to find two ways to take a tennis ball and throw it so that it goes a short distance, then reverses itself and goes the opposite way. You may not bounce the ball off of anything and you may attach nothing to the ball. Can you figure out both ways to do it?

Solution:

1. Throw the ball vertically into the air. It will travel a short way, stop, then reverse direction.

2. Roll it up a hill (ditto).

Day 170

Word of the Day:

adamant (ad´ i mint)

A. Small candy pieces served as dessert
B. An addition to an insurance policy
C. A small broach usually made of ivory or jade
D. Firm, unyielding (adj.)

Use: We tried to talk him out of it, but Bill was *adamant* about driving in the icy weather.

Thought of the Day:

"Miracles are not contrary to nature, but only to what we know of nature."
St. Augustine

Hook:

Project or distribute the figure below. Have the students look at the center of the figure and ask them what begins to happen at the intersections of the white spaces between the blocks.

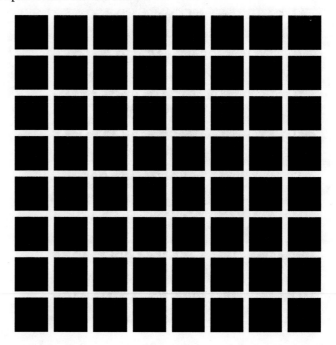

For a full-size reproducible of this image, see Appendix, page 220.

See some gray blocks at the intersections? Hmmmm.

Day 171

Word of the Day:

reticent (ret´ i cent)

Ⓐ Reluctant to speak (adj.)
B. In a rigid, uncompromising manner
C. Blind, unable to see
D. Bankrupt

Derivatives: reticently, reticence
Use: Despite our urging her to voice her opinion, Brittany remained *reticent*.

Thought of the Day:

"You can't steal second base with one foot still on first." *Satchel Paige*

Hook:

Following are three unusual anagrams. Not only can these phrases be rearranged to form new words, but those words are the opposite (well, sort of) in meaning to the phrases as they now exist. See if your kids can figure them out:

1. More tiny

2. I limit arms

3. Fine tonic

Solution:

1. Enormity

2. Militarism

3. Infection

Day 172

Word of the Day:

quiescent (quee es´ ent)

A. Inactive, dormant (adj.)
B. Agreeable
C. Nauseous, sick
D. Transparent

Derivatives: quiescently, quiescence
Use: The volcano, after months of uneasy rumblings, returned to a *quiescent* state.

Thought of the Day:

"Technology is simply the means by which we arrange the world so we no longer have to experience it." *William James*

Hook:

See if you can trip up your students with this one. You have four letters and four envelopes, but you are not sure which letter goes in which envelope, so you simply choose envelopes randomly and seal all the letters. What are the mathematical odds that you will have only three letters in the right envelopes?

Solution:

Zero. If three are correct, the fourth must also be correct.

Day 173

Word of the Day:

cavalier (cav a leer´)

- Ⓐ Carefree, reckless (adj.)
- B. Speedy
- C. Cautious, careful
- D. An explorer of caves

Derivative: cavalierly
Use: Aaron's *cavalier* attitude made it obvious he was not going to be one of our better volunteers.

Thought of the Day:

"If we cannot now end our differences, at least let us make the world safe for diversity." *John F. Kennedy*

Hook:

Three more number/letter combinations to decode:

1. 26 C E the L of the A

2. A P is W 1,000 W

3. 29 D in F in a LY

Solution:

1. 26 cubits equals the length of the ark

2. A picture is worth 1,000 words

3. 29 days in February in a leap year

Day 174

Word of the Day:

benevolent (be nev´ a lent)

A. Wise
B. Charitable, kindly (adj.)
C. Ignorant
D. Out of touch, badly dated

Derivatives: benevolently, benevolence
Use: The woman's sincerity and warmth reflected her *benevolent* nature.

Thought of the Day:

"Patience—the windmill never strays in search of the wind." *Andy Skilvis*

Hook:

You have a full 8-gallon cask of wine. You have a 5-gallon bucket and a 3-gallon bucket. Neither the cask nor the buckets are calibrated in any way. How can you measure precisely 4 gallons into each bucket?

Solution:

	Cask	3 gal.	5 gal.
Pour 5 gallons into 5 gallon bucket	3	0	5
Pour 3 gals from 5 to 3	3	3	2
Pour 3 gals from 3 to cask	6	0	2
Pour 2 gals from 5 to 3	6	2	0
Pour 5 gals from cask to 5	1	2	5
Pour 1 gal from 5 to 3	1	3	4
Pour 1 gal from cask to 3	0	4	4

Day 175

Word of the Day:

askance (a skance´) or *askant* (a skant´)

A. Pertaining to a scarcity
B. To view with skepticism or suspicion (adv.)
C. Pertaining to a graceful dance step
D. Unfaithful, especially in marriage

(B is circled)

Use: He looked *askance* at the hurriedly thrown together plan.

Thought of the Day:

"If men rule the world, why don't they stop wearing neckties?" *Linda Ellerbee*

Hook:

Write clues 1–6 on the board and read the rest. I have 20 boxes labeled 1–20. In one box is a prize, but I only get one chance to get the right box. I asked six people for some information that will help me find the right box. Here are their answers:

1. It's in an odd-numbered box.
2. It's in an even-numbered box.
3. It's in a box whose number is double digits.
4. The number of the box has a 1 in it.
5. The number of the box is a multiple of 3.
6. The number of the box is between 6 and 13.

There is a problem. One, and only one, of them is lying. Which box should I open?

Solution:

Actually there are several ways to figure it out. Here is one:

Either 1 or 2 is the liar since they can't both be true. From 3, 4, and 6 we know it's a double-digit number between 6 and 13 with a 1 in it—this narrows it to 10, 11, or 12 and only twelve is a multiple of 3. Ergo, I should take box 12.

Day 176

Word of the Day:

zephyr (zef´ er)

A. A hot air or gas filled aerial balloon
B. A light breeze (noun)
C. A passenger train
D. A small mammal of Southeast Asia

Use: The *zephyr* was a welcome relief from the hot afternoon sun.

Thought of the Day:

"It's easier to understand a nation by listening to its music than by learning its language." *Anon*

Hook:

Bennie has a chain of seven links. He has promised Trish that he will give her a link on the first day, two links on the second day, three on the third, etc., until she has all seven links. But the links are currently bound together. How many cuts will Bennie have to make in the chain in order to be able to give Trish an additional link each day? (No, not seven.)

Solution:

Cut only link number 3. This will make three lengths of 1, 2, and 4 links. By trading back and forth Bennie can indeed give Trish an ascending number of links each day.

Day 177

Word of the Day:

recapitulate (re ka pit´ chu late)

A. To surrender
B. To vomit
C. To encourage others to try again after an initial failure
D. To summarize (verb)

Derivatives: recapitulation, recapitulative, recapitulatory, recapitulated, recapitulating, recapitulates
Use: Before we begin today's session, I'll ask Anna to *recapitulate* what we accomplished yesterday.

Thought of the Day:

"If you can do it—it ain't braggin'." *Mohammed Ali*

Hook:

Ben says, "All of my pets are rabbits but two, all are parakeets but two, and all are dogs but two. How many animals do I have?"

Solution:

Ben has three animals: one rabbit, one parakeet, and one dog.

Day 178

Word of the Day:

knave (nave)

A. A valve that shuts off the flow of water
B. A crafty, dishonest person (noun)
C. Nerve, daring
D. The small flinted wheel that sparks to ignite a cigarette lighter

Derivatives: knavish, knavery, knavishly, knavishness

Use: His pretense was soon unraveled and instead of the man we thought he was, we realized he was nothing more than a *knave*.

Thought of the Day:

"The way I see it, if you want the rainbow, you gotta put up with the rain."
Dolly Parton

Hook:

Susan had some cake left and offered it to Jim and Allan. Both wanted some, but each was afraid the other would get the bigger piece. Susan refused to cut the pieces herself, but she solved the dilemma nicely. What did she do?

Solution:

She told them that one could cut the cake into two pieces, but the other would get first choice of which piece to take.

Day179

Word of the Day:

placate (play´ kate)

A. To weld at extremely high temperatures
B. The printing surface of a printing press
C. To pretend
D. To pacify or assuage (verb)

Derivatives: placated, placates, placating, placater, placation, placatory, placative
Use: Marianne was so upset that all our efforts to *placate* her were for naught.

Thought of the Day:

"We all have to start at the bottom. Just be sure you don't get to like it down there." *Anon*

Hook:

Ron has rowed across the lake with a load of lumber. The agreement is that Chelsea will trade the same weight of corn for the lumber. The problem is that neither Ron nor Chelsea knows how much the lumber weighs and there are no scales of any kind available. How can they make an even trade weight wise?

Solution:

Get Ron out of the boat, then mark the water line on the side of the boat. Unload the lumber and begin loading corn until the mark is again at the water line.

Day 180

Word of the Day:

alleged (a ledged´) or (a ledge´ ed)

(A.) To assert without proof (adj.)
B. Built upon a substantial foundation
C. In the past
D. Caught, apprehended

Derivatives: allege, alleged, alleging, alleges, allegeable, alleger, allegedly
Use: He *alleged* his innocence, though there seemed to be substantial proof otherwise.

Thought of the Day:

"I prefer the errors of enthusiasm to the indifference of wisdom." *Anatole France*

Hook:

"Let us test your deductive powers," said Inspector Davi to his new assistant. "Given the following information, can you deduce the guilty party?"

"I'll certainly try, sir," replied Bromley.

"Very well:
1. The thief, who was one of the three visitors, arrived at the castle earlier than at least one of the other two visitors.
2. The detective, sent to investigate the robbery, was one of the three visitors and arrived at the castle later than at least one of the other two visitors.
3. The detective arrived at midnight.
4. Neither Bowden nor Wilton arrived after midnight.
5. The person who arrived before Chow and Wilton was not the detective.
6. The person who arrived after Bowden and Wilton was not the thief.

Now Bromley, can you tell me who is the thief?"

"Really sir, this hasn't been much of a challenge. I can tell you straight away who is the thief."

Can you?

Solution:

Bowden. From the first two statements we know that the thief had to be the first or second arriver and the detective had to be second or third arriver. The detective was sent to investigate and is therefore himself innocent. From statement 4 we know that the detective must be either Bowden or Wilton, which leaves Chow as the third arriver. From 5 we know that Bowden arrived first and is not the detective. 6 tells us that Chow is innocent and combined with 5 tells us that Wilton is the detective, leaving Bowden as the guilty party.

Appendix

Day 16

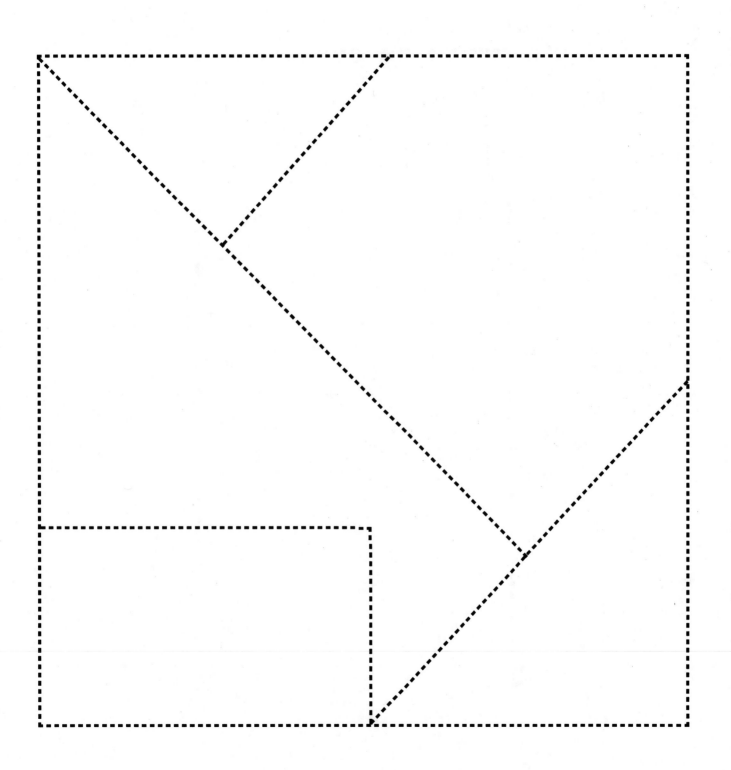

Day 21

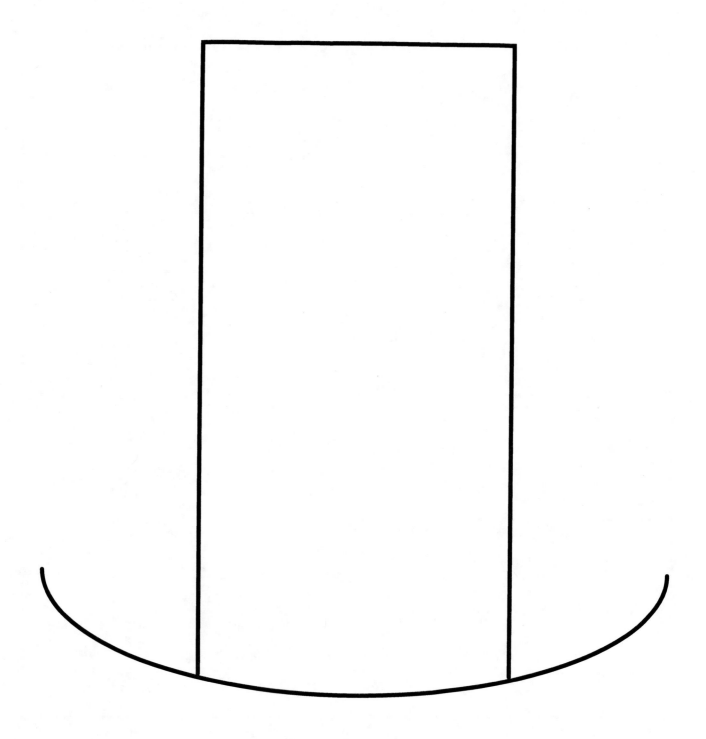

Day 30

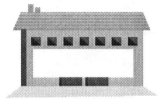

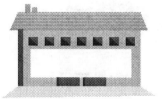

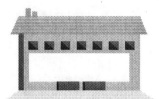

Day 33

Day 46

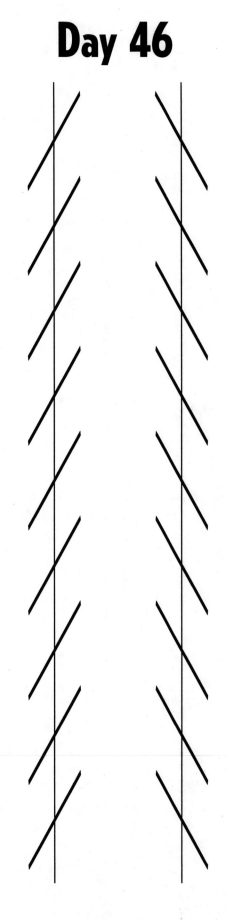

Day 57

Day 73

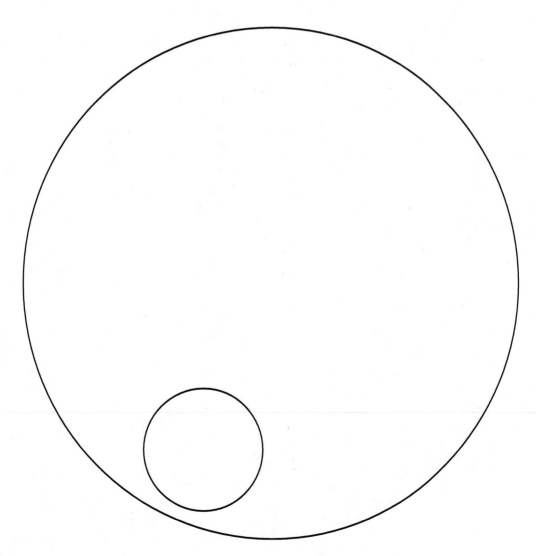

Day 96

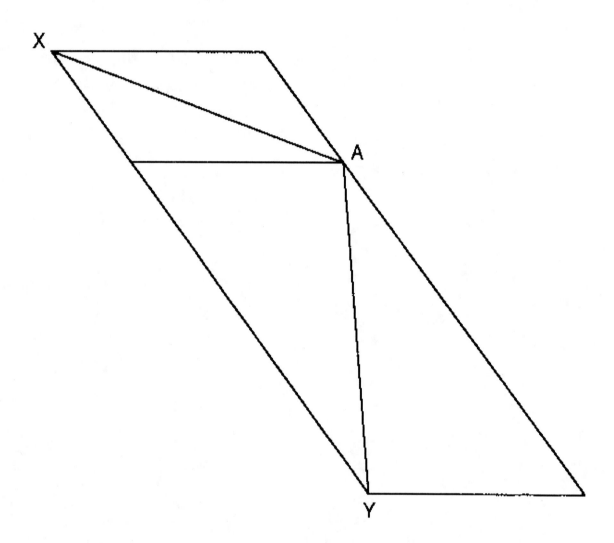

Day 101

You are an agent working for Homeland Security. You have received a tip that a terrorist is aboard Flight 788 that just landed. The following people, about whom you have been given some scanty information, get off the plane. Put a 1 beside the person you would search first, a two beside the person you would search second, etc., until you have numbered all the possible suspects.

_____ **Mrs. Edwina Stanton: White American, age 32, housewife.**

_____ **Dr. Raul Sanchez: Mexican American, age 64, medical doctor**

_____ **Gina LeMay: Black Muslim American, age 28, nurse**

_____ **Hikim Ali Budeen: Saudi, age 22, exchange student**

_____ **Pierre DePew: French, age 36, importer/exporter**

_____ **Jeanie Spencer: White American, age 15, high school student**

_____ **Edmund Wellington: English, age 42, college professor**

_____ **May Ling Chow: Chinese, age 20, exchange student**

_____ **Naomi Mobutto, Nigerian, age 27, fashion designer**

_____ **Alexi Durapov, Russian, age 45, newspaper reporter**

When you are finished, set the first list aside. Now, rank the same people placing a 1 beside the person least like you, a 2 beside the person next least like you, etc. until the list is complete. Then compare lists.

Day 105

You will need a white blank sheet of paper for this illusion. Arrange the white sheet close by. Stare at the figure for 30 seconds and try not to move your eyes or blink. Then, as quickly as possible, shift your gaze to the white sheet. Give it a second or two and you should see something interesting.

Day 129

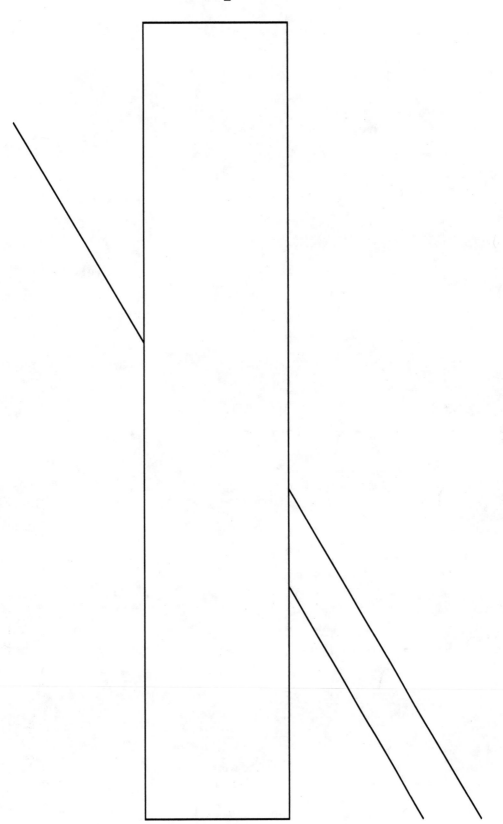

Day 152

Day 170

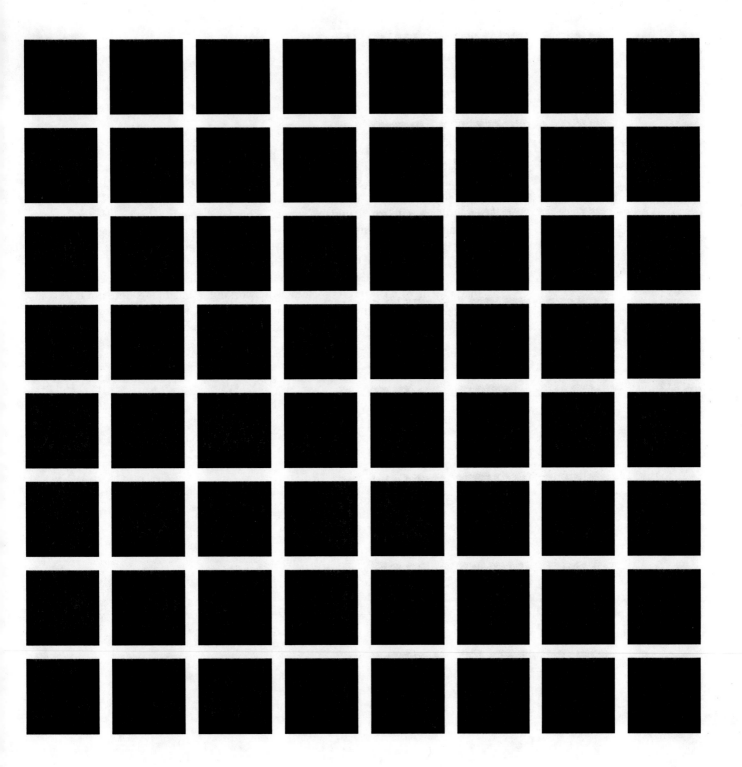

A Personal Note

I hope you have found these 180 hooks of use in getting your classes off to a good start. I'd be very interested in receiving your feedback as to how helpful these have been and whether you found that using hooks and grabbers improved the learning atmosphere in your classroom. Any comments and suggestions will be welcome at:

Steve Young
1570 East Clack Mt. Rd.
Clearfield, KY 40313
bsyoung@mis.net

About the Author

Steve Young recently retired from a 33-year career as a Professor of Education at Morehead State University after first teaching high school English in the public school system. He holds a BA degree in English and MA degree in Education from Morehead State University and Ed.S. and Ed.D. degrees in Instructional Systems Technology from Indiana University. Having previously written a manual for the teaching of decision-making and critical thinking, this is his second work written specifically for the high school and middle school teacher. He has published a novel, *Time in a Bottle*, and is currently finishing two other novels for the popular reading market. His other interests include woodworking, folk singing, and storytelling. He and his wife Barbara live near Morehead, Kentucky, on a ridge top overlooking Daniel Boone National Forest with their two collies.